Analyzing Ethics Questions from Behavior Analysts

Supplementing the best-selling textbook, *Ethics for Behavior Analysts*, this book analyzes over 50 original and up-to-date ethics cases recently faced by behavior analysts. The workbook provides "solutions" to each question written by the most expert professionals in the field using the Behavior Analyst Certification Board® Ethics Code. Covering all ten sections of the code and designed to allow the reader to see the original question, respond given their knowledge of the Code, and then compare their answers with the authors' answers at the back of the book, Jon S. Bailey and Mary R. Burch provide the necessary guided practice for both students and clinicians to improve ethical competency in behavior analysis.

Jon S. Bailey, PhD, Emeritus Professor of Psychology at Florida State University, teaches graduate courses for behavior analysts. Dr. Bailey is a founding director of the Behavior Analyst Certification Board®, past president of the Florida Association for Behavior Analysis, and a fellow of the Association for Behavior Analysis International.

Mary R. Burch, PhD, is a Board-Certified Behavior Analyst®. Dr. Burch has more than 25 years of experience in developmental disabilities. She has been a behavior specialist, QMRP, unit director, and consulting behavior analyst in developmental disabilities, mental health, and preschool settings.

Analyzing Ethics Questions from Behavior Analysts
A Student Workbook

Jon S. Bailey and Mary R. Burch

Routledge
Taylor & Francis Group

NEW YORK AND LONDON

First published 2019
by Routledge
52 Vanderbilt Avenue, New York, NY 10017

and by Routledge
2 Park Square, Milton Park, Abingdon, Oxon, OX14 4RN

Routledge is an imprint of the Taylor & Francis Group, an informa business

Library of Congress Cataloging-in-Publication Data
Names: Bailey, Jon S., author. | Burch, Mary R., author.
Title: Analyzing ethics questions from behavior analysts : a student workbook / Jon S. Bailey and Mary R. Burch.
Description: New York, NY : Routledge, 2019. | Includes bibliographical references and index.
Identifiers: LCCN 2018047076 (print) | LCCN 2018049146 (ebook) | ISBN 9781351117784 (E-book) | ISBN 9780815353003 (hardback) | ISBN 9780815360698 (pbk) | ISBN 9781351117784 (ebk)
Subjects: LCSH: Behavioral assessment—Moral and ethical aspects—United States—Handbooks, manuals, etc. | Behavior analysts—Professional ethics—United States—Handbooks, manuals, etc.
Classification: LCC RC437.B43 (ebook) | LCC RC437.B43 B353 2019 (print) | DDC 174.20973—dc23
LC record available at https://lccn.loc.gov/2018047076

ISBN: 978-0-815-35300-3 (hbk)
ISBN: 978-0-815-36069-8 (pbk)
ISBN: 978-1-351-11778-4 (ebk)

Typeset in Frutiger
by Apex CoVantage, LLC

Dedication

This book is dedicated to Lee Meyerson, PhD, my research and clinical-behavior-analysis mentor at Arizona State University, who first introduced me to applied ethics in the 1960s. You taught me about clients' right to privacy and confidentiality and you always emphasized treating clients as individuals who always deserve to be treated with dignity and respect. I am forever grateful.

Jon S. Bailey, PhD, BCBA-D

Dedication

Contents

Preface

Ethics for Behavior Analysts, 3rd Edition was published in response to the Professional and Ethical Compliance Code that was issued in 2016 by the Behavior Analyst Certification Board®.[1] This text augmented the Compliance Code with examples of ethics cases that illustrated both the rules and the intent emanating from the new Code. One result of this publication was an increased rate of behavior analysts seeking clarification of many of the elements of the Code. Some of these behavior analysts found their way to the Association for Behavior Analysis International (ABAI) Hotline where the first author has been answering ethics questions for behavior analysts and consumers since 2010. With the permission of these writers, some of their questions, cases, and scenarios have served as teachable instances in presentations at conferences and they have generated considerable interest in the process of analyzing the cases and arriving at answers, guidance, and solutions. As a service to the field, the first author has also been invited to act as a *pro bono* guest speaker in many graduate ethics classes via Skype, Zoom, GoToMeeting, and other platforms. Students are free to ask questions that are relevant to their individual situations. By raising the question about how one goes about arriving at an ethics solution, these discussions sparked the idea of a book explaining how this is carried out.

INTRODUCTION TO *ANALYZING ETHICS QUESTIONS: A WORKBOOK FOR BEHAVIOR ANALYSTS*

Our goal for *Analyzing Ethics Questions: A Workbook for Behavior Analysts* is to provide behavior analysis faculty, students, and practitioners with a framework for analyzing, arriving at, and detailing answers to common questions about ethical practices encountered in their daily work with clients, parents, caregivers, supervisors, and supervisees. For the last several years, the first author has been answering an increasing number of questions via the ABAI Hotline. In 2017, over 1,000 questions were submitted and answered, usually on the same day and often within minutes of being received. Over a period of time spanning several years, in the process of examining the BACB Code of Ethics[2] and answering thousands of ethics questions, the first author has become an *ethicist*. So, what is an ethicist? "An **ethicist** is one whose judgment on ethics and ethical codes has come to be trusted by a specific community, and (importantly) is expressed in some way that makes it possible for others to mimic or approximate that judgment."[3]

A secondary but certainly not unimportant purpose of the book is to alert students and newly initiated Board Certified Behavior Analysts (BCBAs) to the obstacles standing in their way to becoming *ethical* behavior analysts. As you will see from the questions submitted, one major impediment is sometimes a person's employer, or an organization with which they have a consulting arrangement. Some employers have discovered the "cash cow" nature of behavior analysis and want to grow as rapidly as possible in order to generate ever larger profits. Sadly, this is sometimes at the expense of the clients and behavioral staff who are forced to take on more clients and supervisees than they can reasonably manage. The Code of Ethics can be used as a shield against these revenue-oriented pressures.

The workbook is intended as a supplement to *Ethics for Behavior Analysts, 3rd Edition*. The questions cover all ten sections of the Code and are presented in a random manner much as they are received each day via email from the Hotline. The text design of the *Ethics Workbook* is intended to allow readers to view the original question, with space provided to respond given their knowledge of the Code, and then to compare their answers with the author's answers at the back of the book.

ANALYZING QUESTIONS: THE METHOD

The method for responding to questions is fairly simple. There is a "conversation" between the ethicist and each person who writes to the Ethics Hotline about the person's ethical concern by interacting about the elements of the submitted question:

Step One—Overview. Skim the question and determine the overall events that the writer is describing.

Step Two—Determine the Nature of the Request. Try to determine what help the writer is requesting. In some cases, it is confirmation of a conclusion they have already reached, and in others it is clear that they have a sense that what has happened is unethical but they cannot identify the reasons for the ethical problem. In a few cases, the writer has confused or conflated an ethics issue with a legal matter or moral concern.

Step Three—Make the Task Manageable. Start at the beginning and break what is often one long paragraph or long run-on sentence into shorter sentences and paragraphs.

Step Four—Immediate Reactions. Going sentence-by-sentence or paragraph-by-paragraph, the ethicist places notes or comments, asks questions, or simply expresses as immediate emotional reaction, e.g. "an RBT should not be doing this!", "This is not allowed according to the following Code item . . . "

Step Five-A—Analysis and Explanation. Upon discovering that an ethical violation has been described, e.g. "One of the owners is a BCBA and she just hired her daughter who is working on becoming a BCaBA. The owner is supervising her . . . "The ethicist cites the Code item, explains why it is a violation, and tries to provide information on the implications of the ethics violation based on many years of experience in the field of applied behavior analysis.

Step Five-B—Questions that Need Answers. In some cases, there is important missing information or clarifications that are necessary before the ethicist can respond. In these cases, questions are inserted at key junctures in the paragraph and the writer is asked to reply before receiving an opinion. After receiving a reply, the ethicist returns to **Step Five-A** completing the analysis and providing an explanation.

TALK ALOUD PROTOCOL

In the **Response from the Ethicist** for each question shown in the back of the book, the reader is exposed to the five-step working process described above which has similarities to the Talk-Aloud Procedures described in Ericsson, K.A and Simon, H.A (1993) *Protocol Analysis*, "The instruction for talk-aloud asks the subjects to say *out loud* whatever they are saying silently to themselves" p. 226–228. These researchers often used ANAGRAM problem solving or math problems presented to subjects to determine how they arrived at the solutions. So, in the case of ethics problem solving, rather than just reading the question and providing an answer at the end, a "talk-aloud" procedure is used where the ethicist writes immediate responses to each element of the question so that the end result appears similar to a conversation with the writer. This allows the writer to see the decision-making process. Readers of this text should come away with a sense that they can follow this thought process as they work their way through each question whether simple or complex.

HOW TO USE THIS WORKBOOK

The format for the workbook is quite simple. **Section 1** contains over 50 questions that have been submitted over the past six months via the Hotline or from behavior analysts who have attended our presentations at conferences or read *Ethics for Behavior Analysts, 3rd Edition*. They are presented in random order, just as they are received from day to day, so the reader has the same experience as the ethicist—never knowing what question is going to pop up next. The question pages are set up with a wide right margin with lines provided for the reader to provide their immediate reactions, notes, and conclusions. This is on the Honor System—no peeking at the back until you have arrived at your answer! Once you have your best answer, turn to **Section 2** to see the authors' response. You can compare notes and see how closely your answer matched that of the authors. Our hope is that by the time you have worked through a dozen or more questions, your responses will start to resemble those of the behavior-analyst ethicist.

Section 3, Final Words is a recap of key points that readers may want to consider when interviewing for a position as a behavior analyst. These questions have been arrived at as a summary of problems that have been encountered by hundreds of behavior analysts who have written in to the ABAI Hotline.

NOTES

1. © 2015 the Behavior Analyst Certification Board®, Inc. All rights reserved. Reprinted by permission. The most current version of this document is available at www.BACB.com. Contact ip@bacb.com for permission to reprint this material.
2. Code of Ethics and the Code are used synonymously with and short-hand for Professional and Ethical Compliance Codes for Behavior Analysts.
3. Retrieved from Wikipedia 8.6.18.

Acknowledgments

Colleagues both locally and around the country have provided tremendous assistance over the past few years in thinking through issues related to dealing with questions that arrive every day via email. In particular, a heartfelt thank you is due to Tom Zane and Mary Jane Weiss for their willingness to provide a second opinion on complicated problems. They always have a calm and steady approach to even the most unusual questions, they are always honest in their feedback and educational in their responses. Yulema Cruz, PhD candidate at Nova University and active member of the first author's bi-weekly research group, has been a valuable resource for information on issues related to the details of supervision practices and rules. Devon Sundberg, chief executive officer, Behavior Analysis Center for Autism, has provided insight related to ethics issues in a private business. She is always efficient and complete in her answers and responds quickly to a request for help. Finally, with their vast amounts of knowledge pertaining to providing behavioral services, working with agencies, supervising staff and students, and handling ethical issues related to all of these tasks, Al Murphy, Mary Riordan, Lauren Gianino, and Nikki Dickens have also provided invaluable and much appreciated input. And, to the individuals who have contacted me via the ABAI Hotline, I thank you for your trust in me to understand your issues and attempt to provide some assistance. You have given me an advanced course in ethics problem solving. This book is for you.

Disclaimer

This book does not represent an official statement or position by the Behavior Analyst Certification Board®, the Association for Behavior Analysis International, or any other behavior analysis organization. This workbook cannot be relied on as the only interpretation of the meaning of the Professional and Ethical Compliance Codes for Behavior Analysts or the application of the Code to particular situations. Each BCBA®, supervisor, or relevant agency must interpret and apply the Code as it believes proper, given all of the circumstances. The questions used in this text are based on those that have been submitted to the ABAI Hotline, as well as from individuals who have contacted the first author directly, over the past year. In 2017, over 1,000 questions were received and answered, and in 2018, it is expected that there will be an increase in Hotline questions. Some of the questions in this book are nearly verbatim of the actual questions, but in all cases, we have left out or disguised details to protect the privacy of the parties and organizations involved. We do not hold these to be the only correct answers. We encourage instructors who use the text to create alternate solutions based on their own experiences. Finally, we hope that the responses offered here will stimulate discussion, debate, and thoughtful consideration about ways of handling what are by definition very complex and delicate matters involving client treatment as well as supervision issues.

Ethics Questions

ETHICS QUESTION #1

It was brought to my attention that one of my RBTs has a picture of a former client (i.e. no longer receiving services from us) on her phone. The mother of the client sent the picture to the RBT and frequently gives us updates on the child's well-being due to the family moving from one state to another. Is this a violation of Code 2.06 (e)?

I'm assuming this is not a problem since the child is no longer a client; however, I know one ethical code item states waiting two years before having contact with a family who was once in a professional relationship with you (Code 1.07 (b, c) Exploitative Relationships). Yet, this Code item states "sexual relationships" which is definitely not occurring.

ETHICS QUESTION #2

My question is whether a behavior analyst may do a presentation for an advocacy group or a local parent support group for parents of children with some form of disability.

In most cases, one can assume that presenting to a parent group is a problem because parents are "potential users of services who, because of their particular circumstances, are vulnerable to undue influence." I just wanted some clarification.

ETHICS QUESTION #3

I have a quick ethics question. I know that as BCBAs we do not solicit testimonials but is it acceptable to approach a student from the classroom in which I am already working?

I work with a client in a classroom in a school for children with disabilities. There is a peer that I feel could benefit greatly from my services. In the classroom, I have successfully paired him as a peer for my client and have even helped him acquire the beginnings of functional communication in order to facilitate interactions with my client. I would like to offer my services to his mother but I feel like that might not be allowed.

I cannot reason why but it feels like I shouldn't be singling him out of a classroom of children.

What do you think?

ETHICS QUESTION #4

I have an ethics question. I have been at several IEP meetings where a particular individual is using the title of behavior analyst when introducing herself to parents, district representatives, and whoever else is in attendance. This individual is currently collecting her practicum hours and has not yet sat for the exam. I believe she is at 500 hours.

When questioned as to why this individual is representing herself as a behavior analyst, her district is saying that is okay for her to do so because she is in the process of becoming a behavior analyst and that is the job title for which she was hired.

Is it ethical for this person to be calling herself a behavior analyst?

ETHICS QUESTION #5

Dear Behavior Analysis Ethicist,

Thank you for taking the time to read this! I am concerned that I am working for a company that is unethical in its practices, and I am unsure of how to proceed. Some background: I am currently employed as a BCBA by an ABA company that is owned by a pediatric neurologist. Management is pressuring me to implement procedures written by the neurologist that advocate a procedure called "quiet sitting" which requires a child be kept sitting and engaged in absolutely nothing for ten-minute intervals. It does not teach replacement behaviors and the procedure is missing several components of an ethical behavior program.

The clinical director (also a BCBA) is directing me to implement the methods from the book in my ABA programs along with programs that are outside of my scope of practice (OT, speech, academic programs). When I informed management that this is not within my field's Code of Ethics, I was told that I had a narrow-minded interpretation of my ethical code and it may cause me to lose my job.

I found out that children are being restrained during ABA programs that include "quiet sitting." I am unsure if it is best for me to move on to another company or if there is more I should do to advocate for these clients as well as ABA as a whole.

Do you have any suggestions to ensure that I meet my ethical obligations?

ETHICS QUESTION #6

Good evening,

I am an ABA graduate student coming to the end of my degree. As a part of our course, we complete a functional analysis within our supervision setting.

I am also a foster parent. My six-year-old foster daughter who has autism has begun engaging in some worrying behavior at school and at home. I'd like to conduct a functional analysis on the behavior with the support of some fellow students. However, the state has legal custody of her, and I am paid by the state to care for her.

What are my ethical concerns here?

Are they insurmountable?

ETHICS QUESTION #7

I have a concern about a possible ethical violation. I wanted to find out if indeed there has been a violation and what, if anything, I can do about it. I am a BCBA working at an ABA agency. I recently put in my 30-days-notice of resignation, so that I would ideally have enough time to properly transition my cases to another supervisor and say goodbye to my families.

I was called into a last-minute meeting this morning by our executive director, and she handed me my last paycheck and told me that I was to leave the company effective immediately. I was told that I would not be allowed to properly transition my cases to a new supervisor, and I was not allowed to contact any of my families or staff. I had to hand over all documents then and there, and was told to delete all client contact information from my phone. When I asked them why they were doing this, they would not give me a reason. I asked if I had done anything wrong, and they said no.

I told them I felt this was unethical because it seems like client abandonment. I should also note that several BCBAs have put in their resignation recently, and many others are in the process of interviewing elsewhere so there really isn't anyone available to take my clients right now. I am very much concerned for the well-being of my clients and staff, and I do not agree with or feel good about this decision. I feel like this is client abandonment, that I will be leaving staff with no notice or support.

In this situation, was there an ethical violation and is there anything I can do about it?

ETHICS QUESTION #8

I have a 20-year-old client diagnosed with ASD living in a residential setting. I have a behavior plan in place for his SIB, providing replacement behaviors for the SIB, and dealing with his whining. When he doesn't get his way or if a promised reinforcer is not delivered quickly enough, he will whine persistently and can become aggressive. He is about to undergo various treatments for suspected Lyme Disease, Candida infestation (fungal infection), etc. and the interventions are expected to have an impact on MOs and SDs.

The parents have sought out a naturopath (alternative medicine practitioner) for the treatment of the yeast infection without consulting the behavior team. I am unable to work directly with the naturopath because he doesn't want to collaborate and the parents are okay with this. I'm trying to find a comfortable way to look at this but so far, I haven't landed anywhere.

I'm told that the expected impact of being Candida-free is that behavior is likely to change. Specifically, that if there is no more problem behavior it'll be because of the Candida removal. But if there still is problem behavior, there is probably still Candida. And, of course, they're expecting discomfort in the Candida "removal process."

After reviewing the state of the science on these things and asking for the naturopath to add any more info and getting no reply, I am at a bit of a loss. It feels like possible crossroads in treatment planning and implementation on the horizon.

Since this is an adult and the funds are public, there is no real limit as it's one of the "special circumstances" cases meaning that the money is going to flow and they could probably do dolphin therapy if they wanted and get it paid for.

However, I am wondering where things like substitute decision-maker status of guardian would come into question if the treatments are not evidence-based. And whether I would say that and how.

Thank you for any ideas you may have.

ETHICS QUESTION #9

My kindergarten-aged client has an IEP meeting scheduled for tomorrow. We received a draft of the Functional Behavior Assessment (FBA) and Behavior Intervention Plan (BIP) last night. I read in the BIP that the school is using a seclusion room called a "calm-down room," which the mother told me is a padded closet with a locked door.

I find this to be extremely concerning and unethical.

Do we have any procedures in place for reporting or discouraging the use of this type of punishment procedure in public school settings?

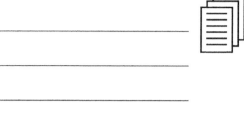

ETHICS QUESTION #10

I am a brand new BCBA who did not receive very good supervision when I was in training, but want to become a responsible supervisor. My company is headed by a BCBA who has supported me, but she does not actually work with clients and she is not up to date on the Code of Ethics.

I was reading through Code 5.0 and was puzzled by 5.07 where it says, "Behavior analysts design systems for obtaining ongoing evaluation of their own supervision activities." I don't know exactly what this means. I've asked the other BCBA who has been here a while and she didn't know either but she told me not to worry about it.

Can you tell me what this means and what I need to do to be compliant? I don't want to be in trouble with the BACB on my first job.

ETHICS QUESTION #11

Hi!

I have a question regarding graduate programs and written academic policies and rules for authorship. In my country, an ABAI accredited graduate program in behavior analysis gives all of its master's students these written instructions for their master's theses: "In the event of publication, academic supervisors shall be acknowledged as co-authors." There is no mention of any contribution by the academic supervisors, as most notably mandated by APA and BACB ethical guidelines.

I am thinking of addressing the department directly, and I am wondering if ABAI has any official policy beyond what is stated in the BACB ethical compliance code (such as the guidelines for The International Committee of Medical Journal Editors (ICMJE), The Vancouver-Group, etc.)?

By the way, the majority of the supervisors are not Board Certified Behavior Analysts.

ETHICS QUESTION #12

I teach an Ethics course and we were just reviewing the compliance code. Could you give me any clarification on one of the Code items? In Code 10.02 (b), it talks about the need to report, "Any public health and safety related fines or tickets where the behavior analyst is named on the ticket." Could you give me examples of the types of tickets or fines this is referring to?

ETHICS QUESTION #13

I am the regional manager of an ABA program. I received the following ethics question from one of our BCBAs regarding an RBT on her team.

The RBT's last day is Friday. Today she was given a going away gift from one of her client's preschool teachers. We know better than to take gifts from clients and their families, but we have never been offered a gift from another professional. The RBT refused the gift, but then the gift was placed in her bag when she wasn't looking.

My question is, should we refuse all gifts from families and other professionals, or does this only apply to clients/families?

ETHICS QUESTION #14

I am a BCBA in a school district. I consult with classrooms that serve students with emotional or behavioral disorders. I've been asked by an administrator who is not my supervisor to provide the academic curricula for classroom teachers. I have a teaching credential and I feel that a curriculum that includes functional skills, social-emotional skills, and behavioral skills falls within my scope of knowledge. However, I am having a hard time considering academic curriculum topics including math, social studies, English, and language arts to be within the scope of a BCBA. I am not working as a teacher, only as a BCBA. I have been offering assistance in structuring lessons to help support pro-social behavior and helping to monitor behavior during lessons.

I was hoping for some assistance in determining whether or not curriculum development is within the scope of a BCBA. I have looked at the Task List for BCBAs and don't see anything remotely close to providing academic curricula for classroom teachers.

ETHICS QUESTION #15

Is there a clear-cut time when the BACB should get involved when an ethics violation has been made? For example, if I see a colleague (fellow BCBA) accept coffee at a client's house (a violation of Code 1.06 (d)), is this something I should report to the BACB? I'm guessing the answer to this is no.

What if behavioral treatment is begun without consent? There is a real possibility of harm here, so I'm guessing maybe?

Where is the line?

ETHICS QUESTION #16

Greetings! I find myself in a difficult situation and am wondering whether it falls into the realm of an ethical violation (albeit potentially minor) or simply poor professional etiquette.

I am in the process of identifying an appropriate home ABA provider for a family in our district. The family currently consults with a psychologist who is also a BCBA. The BCBA provides consultation regarding a medical desensitization program for their child and to assist the family in improving their communication with the school district.

While I was working with two providers to determine which would be the best fit with the student, the psychologist/BCBA, without any request from the school district to do so, sent an email to the entire educational team informing us that he/she had spoken to a former colleague who was a different home ABA provider about the case. The psychologist/BCBA said that this provider was available to take on the student's services. The family is now demanding that this colleague-provider be contacted. I am very concerned the family will not accept any provider that isn't the one recommended by their outside BCBA. In the meantime, the home services that were available to start next week are on hold while I contact this unsolicited provider.

In this case, did the psychologist/BCBA act unethically, violating 2.04 (a), acting outside of their role on the educational team, and potentially violating 1.06, engaging in a possible multiple relationship with this home provider while still working with the family? Or was the psychologist/BCBA simply unprofessional in suggesting a different provider, thus adding conflict to an already charged dynamic?

ETHICS QUESTION #17

Dear Ethics Hotline:

I ran across a BCBA on the internet who is advertising himself as certified in "Astronaut Training." At first blush, that seemed cool. But, upon investigation, I learned that this form of "Astronaut Training" is simply another hyped-up version of sensory integration therapy. With Astronaut Training, clients sit on boards that spin slow or fast, while the therapist plays fake "space-sounding music." It is totally bogus in my opinion—look it up yourself.

Several things bother me: (1) It appears that there is no peer-reviewed research to support Astronaut Training; (2) Astronaut Training is derived from *sensory integration therapy*, which has little to no empirical support; (3) the conceptualization of behavior from a sensory integration perspective is diametrically opposite of our (behavior analysis) conceptualization of behavior; (4) by practicing this method, this BCBA is NOT putting behavior analysis above all other professions which I think is some kind of violation of our Code of Ethics.

This BCBA doesn't seem to be adhering to what he has learned in grad school about evidence-based practice. Plus, his clients to whom he delivers this astronaut training are not receiving "effective treatment."

What should I do?

ETHICS QUESTION #18

I am looking at the possibility of beginning to offer remote supervision within my country (Australia) and I would like to know how the supervisory relationship relates to the supervisee's clients.

In Australia, there is a likelihood that some potential supervisees will be working independently or for companies that do not have Behavior Analysts on staff, which means there will likely be a high variability in service delivery. I am concerned that since supervisors are required to observe their supervisees working directly with clients during each supervisory period, the supervisor's responsibility will be extended to the quality and safety of the supervisee's clients as well.

What level of responsibility do supervisors have to the clients of an independent supervisee?

ETHICS QUESTION #19

Knowing that they are not evidence-based, should BCBAs be implementing treatments such as Zones of Regulation, and Social Behavior Mapping as treatments for children with autism?

Is this issue one that should be brought to the Board for review?

ETHICS QUESTION #20

I am a parent and I have a question regarding ethics when it comes to charging fees. My wife and I recently reached out to a behavior analyst for our son who has been diagnosed with mild autism. The therapist sent us her fee schedule and we scheduled a phone-intake interview. We knew we were being charged for this interview, but I should make it clear that we have never signed anything saying that we understand how her fees work. She then proceeded, with our permission, to observe our son at school. We knew we would be charged for this as well. She also consulted with numerous other people on our son's team (teachers, speech therapist etc.). Her fee schedule mentioned that she charges for any consultation time above 15 minutes. Before contacting these people, she never reminded us of this nor did she ask how long we would give her permission to be on the phone at our expense. We were not present for these phone calls so we had no control and she did not make the people being consulted aware of the charges.

She has now charged us a large sum for these calls as well as her calls to us beyond the initial phone interview. Basically, she has charged us for consultations that went beyond what we would have given her permission for had we been informed properly of this charge AND she is charging us for getting information on our child. This is a form of ransom, isn't it?

I am also a teacher and I know that my principal wouldn't dream of charging parents for teacher contact. It's expected, it's part of the job. We have spoken to numerous other BCBAs who have informed us that the above practices of this behavior therapist are not the standard. So, I guess my question is: Has this behavior therapist broken anything in your Code of Ethics? If she has, what can we do? We will not be continuing with this therapist as her hidden expectations have put a bad taste in our mouths.

ETHICS QUESTION #21

I had a question surrounding consent. I cannot seem to find an appropriate answer that directly cites the Professional and Ethical Compliance Code in some way. I am assuming that I should just err on the side of caution, anyway, but I would like to hear your opinion on the topic.

I have been a BCBA for one year now. I currently work for a company that contracts with schools for consultation, supervision, and assessment needs for multiple disciplines (BCBAs, School Psychologists, LICSWs, ABA therapy, testing services, etc.). I have a school that I am contracted with for 12 hours per week. Within this BCBA consultation, I complete any FBAs that the school needs conducted, and my remaining hours will be dedicated to helping observe and making suggestions for any students that they may be struggling with. For the FBAs, my company typically completes a separate Letter of Agreement and/or the schools receive a signed informed consent surrounding the assessment before I begin.

My question is, for the other students that they are requesting me to "help out" with, is it necessary that I also receive parental consent for observation and any plans suggested thereafter? Or do I operate under the premise that I am acting as a school employee and already have some kind of inherent consent? (I am unsure if a district-employed BCBA would need consent for these things, as well, as compared to my position as more of a "third party" contract). At which point in the consultation process does the school BCBA need consent to observe a particular student? Would it be after observing, if further functional assessment and formal behavior plans are warranted? Or does the BCBA need a consent simply to observe? Does this situation differ from a permanently hired district employee compared to my role as an outside contract employee?

My company is trying to research the correct direction to take this. With multiple disciplines hired within, it would be important that each employee understands their obligation for obtaining consent, and if they need to delegate this responsibility to the schools before proceeding with any interaction with the student.

ETHICS QUESTION #22

I'm writing to you because I'm facing an ethical issue in my practice that I'm not sure how to handle. Over the past two months, through my place of work (an integrated preschool/ABA service provider), I have met with two families who would like to enroll their children in our program. Both of these families are currently receiving services from another ABA service provider, which is owned and operated by a BCBA.

Both of these families have volunteered information about the other service provider that I know conflicts with the Professional and Ethical Compliance Code. Neither set of parents were made aware of what these codes are or how they can lodge a complaint. They are not aware that they have any options for recourse. My own BCBA supervisor (I'm not yet certified) has said that in those situations I can't directly explain to the parents how to lodge a complaint against their previous service provider. I can explain our policies here (which include informing parents of the code and explaining how to lodge a complaint), and leave it at that. If the parents decide to use this information to lodge a complaint against their previous service provider, then that is beyond my area of concern.

The thing I'm struggling with is this: At what point do the ethical violations I'm hearing about constitute enough of a problem that I, as a practitioner, have an ethical duty to intervene? These aren't small problems that I could solve with a gentle reminder to this BCBA. Complaints include shady billing practices, charging for services the parents haven't consented to, requiring parents to enroll in services outside the scope of ABA, not providing services that meet the standards for best practice, and one occasion where a child was hurt and they didn't follow proper protocol. This is not even a complete list of the issues that have been brought to my attention by these parents.

I am conflicted because I know that I can't directly instruct these parents to make a complaint. However, I know that the likelihood of them initiating this process on their own is minimal, and this practitioner is still providing service to families and children in my city.

Any guidance would be greatly appreciated!

ETHICS QUESTION #23

I was recently excluded from authorship on a published paper on which I was supposed to be an author.

I contacted the primary author and he said he would confirm I am an author if anyone ever questioned it. Is that the correct form of action when excluding an author from a published paper?

ETHICS QUESTION #24

About a week ago, I met a person at a local autism fundraiser and he asked for my business card. When he saw that I am a BCBA, he commented on my credentials and said he is taking his exam in November.

He gave me his card and I didn't look at it until recently. He has his name followed by, BCBA(C). I feel like he is misrepresenting himself as a BCBA when he hasn't taken his exam yet and I've never heard of BCBA(C).

Do I need to report this to the BACB?

_____

_____

_____

_____

_____

_____

_____

_____

_____

_____

_____

_____

_____

_____

_____

_____

_____

_____

ETHICS QUESTION #25

There is a colleague who lives in the US and is Brazilian. She comes back to Brazil every now and then to teach "workshops" and constantly posts pictures from these workshops and the people who attend them on Facebook.

In addition, on her Facebook page, she frequently posts pictures with supervisees and students.

She also uses the BACB stamp when disseminating her workshop fliers. It appears that she is using the BACB's name to give her workshop an increased value or strength.

I have heard (but have no proof) that she has been publicizing that she is the only one in Brazil who can offer services based on Applied Behavior Analysis.

Last year, one of her fliers stated she was a PhD. I wrote her to ask her to remove that information because she only has a master's degree.

People write me every week to let me know of something she has done, but I keep saying that if someone wants to report something they should write to the BACB.

My question is: Given everything that is on her Facebook page (this is the only thing I have access to), should I report this person?

ETHICS QUESTION #26

Here is my question: Information for an upcoming school training has been disseminated. A well-known BCBA is the contact person. The training is on Social Thinking, which does not have a solid research base but is frequently used in the autism treatment community.

The BCBA is only responsible for taking questions and issuing CE credit for the professional development/training. I'm unsure how much she was involved in the decision-making process prior to the training announcement (i.e. whether she recommended the curriculum, was involved in the conversations of whether or not it is evidence-based, how to advertise, etc.).

I have been in contact with the BCBA to see if there was a way for her to distance herself from the training. Because we are in such a small state/community, even if she were not to use her BCBA credential, everyone knows she is a BCBA. She indicated that it would not be her place to provide a disclaimer that the curriculum is not evidence-based. I have since asked if there would be a way for her to no longer be the contact person. My concern is that promoting or appearing to promote this curriculum is not being consistent with the BACB Professional and Ethical Compliance Code specifically related to reliance on scientific knowledge (Code 1.01), being conceptually consistent (4.01), affirming principles (6.01), and disseminating behavior analysis (6.02).

What are some reasonable next steps? As I indicated, I am very much aware that the Social Thinking curriculum is very popular in the autism community and that many BCBAs are using it within a solid behavior context (operationally defining terms, taking data, etc.).

Thank you for your time and any guidance you may have.

ETHICS QUESTION #27

Message to the Behavior Analyst Ethicist:

Is asking employees to post a review on a recruitment website unethical? One of my employees expressed a concern so I wanted to check.

I don't know if this is a cut-and-dried question, or if you would like more context. The following is context from my perspective.

Context:

I emailed the entire company with the request and I have not mentioned it since. The website requires reviewers to indicate whether they are current employees. So, there was no subterfuge, I did not tell them what to say or make any statements to insinuate either desirable or undesirable consequences based on their response. Is this ethical?

ETHICS QUESTION #28

I have an ethical situation I would like some advice on to ensure that I am acting appropriately.

Two months ago, I put in my 30-days-notice with my previous company. I worked for the company as a BCaBA assisting the BCBAs. During that notice time, no one from the company contacted me about transitioning a client to a new provider. The company did not even contact the client's parents to schedule transitioning to another 1:1 provider until my final week. On my last day working for the company, an RBT contacted me to ask questions about what she was supposed to do with that client and mentioned him by name. She said she got my phone number from the client's parents. I informed her that I was no longer a contractor with the company and that any programming and treatment decisions needed to come from the current team on the client's case. I told her to ask one of the company owners or the BCBA on the case to discuss with her what needed to be done with the client.

In March 2017, I received a very nasty email from one of the owners, claiming that for three years I've never turned in any session notes and that they were keeping my final paycheck and were going to report me to the "proper agencies." I responded that she needed to check the email messages from early March in which I submitted documentation for all of 2015 through February 2017. I also said that the remainder of the documents had been uploaded into the company database from February until I left the company. In February 2017, the company conducted an internal audit and saw that I was missing documentation. I provided all of the missing documentation that was requested in early March 2017. The owner has not responded to that email. I also saw on my final Year-to-Date statement from early March they withdrew a $100 administrative charge to "upload documentation and notes into the data base."

Later the same day I sent the email in March, I got a call from the executive director who told me that after he read the email that was sent he "knew where this was going" and wanted to intervene. I explained to him that I knew this was just a ploy to try to keep my final paycheck; this is a regular business practice with this company. (I have documentation from previous technicians who've left this company asking me why they did not receive their final paychecks.) I have email correspondence between myself and a co-owner of the company in which I pointed out that immediately after I put in my final notice, an administrator reduced my pay rate by almost $10 an hour for one insurance company, and for a second insurance company they reduced it to $0.00. The co-owner emailed me stating he would fix this. He did not say it was an accident or deny that an administrator went back and illegally adjusted the codes.

It is now June. Yesterday morning, I emailed the executive director to put our phone conversation in written format and to confirm with him that he told me that he "knows it is illegal to try to withhold someone's paycheck" and that he was going to work to settle this as quickly as possible. He has not responded to my email.

Last night, I got a call from another behavior analyst asking me to discuss the same client that the technician called me about. I explained to him that I no longer work for the company and that it would be a HIPAA violation to discuss this client. He stated that the Board (BACB) requires me to work with him to transition this client to him. I stated that the transition was to be done during my 30 days' notice period and he said the company was unable to find anyone until now. At this point, I told him I would contact the BACB for guidance on this situation and would follow any suggestions and recommendations they made.

I'm sorry for this very long message but I feel like I'm being harassed and that they are trying to get me to violate HIPAA as well as to work without pay. I would just like some advice.

ETHICS QUESTION #29

I work in a school district where a parent contacted the BCBA and said she won't consent to the initiation of services. May the BCBA initiate services at school without the parent's consent if directed to do so by the school district?

_____

_____

_____

_____

_____

_____

_____

_____

_____

_____

_____

_____

_____

_____

_____

_____

_____

_____

_____

ETHICS QUESTION #30

I am a BCBA and I co-own an ABA company in the Southeast. I was previously working for another company in the area as a case supervisor. We'll call the company "Company A." Although I never signed a formal contract with Company A, one of the co-owners of my current company signed a contract that pertains to BCBAs. This contract was very vague, but there was a non-compete clause in this contract.

We have not been soliciting previous clients in any way, but over the past few months I have had almost all of my clients independently contact us about leaving Company A and coming to our new company. We initially turned away these clients because we wanted to make sure legally and ethically we are not taking clients from our previous company too quickly. We have been referring these clients to another provider in the area because they are not happy with the services being provided at Company A. We have told them truthfully why we feel we can't take them as clients at this time. Some of the clients have chosen to wait until we are ready to take former clients at our new company. We told them we will keep them updated about when we are able to do this.

Our biggest question is what a safe time limit would be to take on these new clients. We have some parents that are very upset and are having a hard time understanding why they can't choose which provider their child and their family uses. It is like the families are indirectly under a non-compete! This has been a hard question for me to answer.

We have consulted a few different lawyers and they have looked at different cases under our state law. It seems that this subject is very up in the air. I know health providers are generally not able to be held under non-competes in court, and I'm not sure if we would technically be considered health providers as BCBAs. Have you run into this in another situation? We are also looking for guidance on what to tell families. It's hard to turn these families away when they're clearly not happy with their current provider.

Another question we have is about Google and Facebook reviews. We are very familiar with our ethical code when it comes to testimonials and reviews. When trying to boost our site optimization in order to show up on search engines, we have read that a big component is having reviews on Google, Facebook, etc. We know that current clients can never give us reviews and that reviews have to specify if they're solicited or unsolicited. Is there an ethical way for us to still have reviews on Google/Facebook? We have been turning the reviews off, or reporting them to have them removed. I have noticed that other providers have reviews. Of course, complying with our ethical code would be our number one priority, even if that means we're a little lower on the Google search! We are wondering if we can still have reviews.

ETHICS QUESTION #31

I hope this email finds you well. I am reaching out once again, as your guidance and suggestions in the past have worked tremendously.

I am a BCBA and business owner of an ABA clinic in South Florida. Unfortunately, I have received four resignations within the past month, and some of the staff have said that they're being offered $10+ an hour over what I am offering and some are Independent Contractor positions. With the first resignation, I began completing an exit interview asking what we could have done better and what made them decide to resign, so I am hoping to make some future changes to my business.

However, I am a bit concerned, since I have been participating in a Facebook group where this has been discussed and many people have expressed the high rates of burnout in the field recently. My question to you is: Can RBTs be classified as Independent Contractors or should they be all employees regardless of the number of hours worked per month?

I ask because I've heard mixed responses from those on the Facebook group, so I am unsure what we should be doing legally.

Your guidance will be much appreciated!

ETHICS QUESTION #32

Our agency has not been involved in formal IRB-approved research at this point in time, however, one of our BCBAs took a strong interest in a particular topic and sought out an expert in our field in that area. This expert ended up asking if our BCBA would be interested in helping generalize his results into natural settings (as we have many BCBAs placed in public schools where this research hasn't been conducted yet) saying our staff could be first author on the article. He was able to add one of her cases onto an existing IRB approval and then set up one of his doctoral students to support her in implementing this. So far, this has only been through phone support. Our BCBA has attended several of the expert's training sessions over the last two years. The BCBA has done a lot of implementation related to the topic and has read the limited amount of research the expert has published. We thought the doctoral student was going to be present with the BCBA to run IOA. However, after having already started the project, the expert indicated that our staff could only move forward with the research/IRB work if we paid him to do an intensive and expensive training session he would conduct because he can't publish anything without first saying that the person running it is well trained.

We certainly agree that fidelity is crucial as is training, however, we are questioning if this is now creating a bias and crosses some ethical lines. Paying the expert to do this would create a different vested interest in the positive results. His IRB approvals are all run through a university, but it is a bit unclear if this training is just his own or run through the university as well.

Am I overanalyzing this? I was just a bit taken aback and felt we were teased along and once we were engaged in the project, the expert began looking for a sale rather than doing research. Additionally, if he is serious about this, wouldn't he want to send himself or someone he knows is competent in all of this out to run IOA rather than just having us do all of it alone? Is he requiring the training for that reason and it's normal for people to pay to be able to execute research? I'm concerned after paying all this money, he can then turn around and up sell us again by saying our staff wasn't demonstrating competency and needs to do further training for more money.

ETHICS QUESTION #33

I have a question concerning the ethics of accepting or discharging clients from ABA services.

I am taking over the caseload of another BCBA and I have a new-to-me client. The client is an adolescent male who receives a low number of service hours (two per week). He has been working on an eye-contact program for a year with his first BCBA and has not made progress. Last week, he made a gun threat at school and was suspended pending a psychological evaluation. The evaluation has already been done but we have not received any results.

In the past, this client has made similar threats in the clinic regarding our staff. I have not witnessed this but multiple techs have reported it. The majority of the line techs are now afraid to work with him, and to be honest, I don't blame them. I don't want to over- or under-react to this.

Is it ethical to refer the client for psychological services given his lack of progress on his goals here? He has not officially been transferred to my caseload yet, and before this incident I had ideas for changes to his programming that might increase his success. Now I'm wondering if ABA is right for him, and also whether recent events in the news are clouding my clinical judgment. Please advise!

ETHICS QUESTION #34

I witnessed a BCBA behave physically aggressive toward my student. She crossed his arms over his body while he was on the ground and when he got up his lips were blue. I am not sure which ethical code this violates, if any. I need guidance on proper documentation and how I can go about reporting her.

ETHICS QUESTION #35

Message to the Ethicist:

I wanted to see if something could be considered "more or least restrictive" in a scenario I encountered this week.

We have monthly fire drills for our office building, which houses a small ABA clinic. Most of our clients have behavioral issues that require exclusionary timeout for the safety of themselves and the staff. The clients are all very skilled at what to do when fire alarms go off and how to conduct themselves as long as staff are with them and able to model appropriate exiting.

This week, when we had a fire drill, one of my clients was in seclusion and was not ready to come out. She was engaging in a lot of physical aggression toward others when approached. We normally give her a few minutes until calm, then resume her schedule, and she is fine. However, the drill happened right after she went into seclusion. We then were faced with the dilemma of having to get her outside, as we were told by our company that this was something that was "non-negotiable."

I know that in a true emergency (which we knew this was not), we would do whatever it took to get the client(s) out of the building to safety, unless unable to do so. I also know that due to my learning history with this client that the skill is in her repertoire, and she will follow directions to engage in fire drill behavior appropriately when not in seclusion.

However, that day, we had to do something with which I did not feel comfortable. We had to physically move a client that (according to the functional assessment) finds physical touch highly aversive. Because she would not put on her shoes, we had to pick her up and carry her outside with no shoes, and then bring her back into our building for the sake of a fire drill. All this because we were told to. I don't think this falls into "least restrictive practice" and abuses our use of restraint and safety training unless warranted for the safety of the individual and staff. Am I on the right track here or completely off base?

I appreciate your insight in advance!

ETHICS QUESTION #36

I have heard a lot of different opinions on an ethical question that I have, and I was wondering if you could help.

It is my understanding that companies cannot post pictures of their clients to social media or their websites. Ethical guideline 2.06 (e) mentions that we must not share any identifying information (written, photographic, or video) about current clients or supervisees within social media contexts. This seems like a very clear indication that photos are not allowed to be shared.

However, I continue to see many companies posting pictures of their clients on social media and on their websites. I reached out to a behavior podcast and they gave me this response: "Thank you for talking about ethics in social media. As per our ethical guidelines (8.04), companies can post client photos to company website/social media accounts only if they do not use the client's first and last name and written consent for that specific purpose has been obtained."

For testimonials, 8.05 states that behavior analysts should not use testimonials from current clients. If a testimonial is used, a disclaimer should include that the client is a former client, whether it was solicited or unsolicited, and include an accurate description of the current relationship between the company and the testimonial (if there is a current one).

This is very different from our previous guidelines (before January 2016). Many behavior analysis companies are slowly working on making sure their marketing meets the ethical guidelines. Companies have the responsibility to work with their marketing teams to make sure that marketing is adhering to the ethical guidelines (even if marketing doesn't agree!).

Can a company post pictures of clients to social media/website as long as there is written consent and no identifying information?

ETHICS QUESTION #37

Good evening. I am reaching out for guidance regarding an ethical situation in which I am finding myself. I recently transitioned two clients onto my caseload from another BCBA that gave notice at our company. When I transitioned these clients and reviewed their cases, I found multiple ethical violations had occurred.

Looking at the Ethics Code for reporting violations, my first course of action is to try and resolve the matter with that BCBA. I have reached out to review and discuss the violations; however, as the BCBA is no longer a part of our company and cannot remedy the situation, I am unsure what would be considered "resolved" in this case.

I greatly appreciate any guidance in this situation. Thank you in advance for your time and consideration.

ETHICS QUESTION #38

During the past three weeks, my boss has been acting very unusual (extreme lethargy and not remembering conversations or events to the point where clients and parents have noticed). Parents have approached staff due to the concern that he has been under the influence while seeing and transporting their children.

Today, I found a bottle of mixed pills (Vyvanse and Hydrocodone) prescribed to someone (who none of the staff have ever heard of) hidden in a child's wipe container. When staff requested a meeting, our boss refused to meet until his attorney was available via phone. He claimed the pills belonged to a current client who is seen at 7pm by himself at the office. Our administrator for billing has never seen this name before.

Where do I go from here? Do I contact the police to have them discard the pills?

ETHICS QUESTION #39

I work in the Middle East and people here love giving gifts/food. Specifically, when professionals such as behavior analysts go to a home session, the parents will often bring out elaborate food/snacks, etc.

I'm just wondering how this fits with the BACB Ethics Code items 1.06 (d), "Behavior analysts do not accept any gifts from or give any gifts to clients because this constitutes a multiple relationship" and Code 7.01 which says, "Behavior analysts promote an ethical culture in their work environments and make others aware of this Code."

I work in a center where we provide ABA services to children. We have therapists who primarily deliver 1:1 ABA services. Most of these therapists don't have credentials from the BACB and they are not planning to become certified as BCBAs in the near future.

We have supervisors who are BCBAs and they oversee the cases.

Does this "not receiving gifts" Code apply to the frontline therapist even they are not certified by the Board?

Or does the BCBA have the ethical responsibility to promote this "not receiving gifts" to the frontline staff?

ETHICS QUESTION #40

As a behavior analyst, I am deeply invested in the implementation of evidence-based practices with roots it ABA. As an administrator for a school district, I have recently become immersed in a situation for which I'd love to receive your input.

In my little area of California, there has been a surge of families that are embracing Rapid Prompting Method (RPM) and Spelling to Communicate (S2C). As an outside observer, the premise of RPM and S2C look reminiscent of the Facilitated Communication days with the exception being that now the "communication partner" is holding the spelling board rather than touching the student.

In our community, parents have initially implemented RPM and S2C in the home, but in more recent weeks, I'm learning of requests to train school staff to implement these techniques and now, I've received a parent request for their child to receive cognitive/achievement testing with a "communication partner." We have no simple way of identifying whether it is the child or communication partner responding to the questions on the standardized test. In my town, there is even a nonpublic school hoping to open in the fall touting these principles.

I'm reaching out to you because I'm curious if ABAI will be taking a more visible stance regarding RPM/S2C practices and the potential harmful effects of implementation. In compiling information to best prepare myself for parent requests, I found ABAI's 1995 Statement on Facilitated Communication. I'm extremely hopeful that ABAI is considering taking a similar stance on RPM/S2C and if so, if there is a task force currently looking into this more.

ETHICS QUESTION #41

I was approached by a student today whose employer has a policy that requires that all publications/conference presentations by the student both be approved by the company administration *and* include the name of the company as the student's primary affiliation. This is irrespective of if the work is done on company paid time or uses the resources of the company. In addition, the company requires the student to present their proposed talk to the administrators of the company before going to the conference to present it, and the administrator has the right to disapprove the presentation or make changes.

While I am unaware of anything specific to this question in "The Code," I see this situation as being similar to the section dealing with authorship where in this case, having a supervisor who was not involved in a project insisting that his or her name and affiliation be on a publication or presentation.

Finally, the company has a policy that establishes anything done by the employee becomes the "intellectual property" of the company. It doesn't matter if this is done on paid time or the employee's own time.

The point here is that we have many students who conduct research as part of their graduate training and outside the scope of their employment. In my opinion, the products of student/employee work completed under the supervision of their academic advisor should *not* somehow automatically be claimed as the property of the company.

Being an employee does not give the employer the right to claim ownership of the work of the student/employee 24/7.

ETHICS QUESTION #42

I am an ABA therapist working with children with ASD in Europe. I am contacting you as I have an ethical issue related to my professional practice.

I was contacted recently by the mother of a child I worked with for a few years as a home-based therapist. The family moved to the US a few months ago. The mother just informed me that she and the father are currently in the process of divorce. The father requests 50–50 custody over the child, but she would like to limit his custody to a minimum as she believes he cannot fully assume his role as a father and an educator of a child with autism. The mother believes that the father might compromise their child's ABA therapy as he has always shown to be reluctant to ABA and to the suggestions made by different professionals.

The mother asked me, as well as other therapists who have worked with the child, to write a document sharing our observations about the role each parent played during the years we worked with the family. She hopes that this letter might speak in her favor to get custody.

I think a diplomatic way in this situation is to write a document which aims to provide my observations about the progress the child made during the years of ABA therapy he received and to recommend the implementation of this approach in the future, without going into specifics about the parents and defending the position of one parent.

The next step will be to communicate this document to the relevant party. The mother asked me to send it to the forensic psychologist she hired and to her lawyer.

I am not sure how to proceed in this situation. I am afraid that sending them the document will automatically mean that I defend the mother's position and it would force me to respond to any additional questions they may have.

As I have never been confronted with this kind of situation as a therapist, I need some advice about what would be the appropriate way to respond in respect to the behavior analysts' ethical code.

ETHICS QUESTION #43

I have a question regarding the use a of ABA client photos on company webpages. Specifically, I learned in my graduate studies for ABA that client photos could never be used on a webpage as this is a violation of confidentiality. In the code, there seems to be two recommendations regarding this. One, Code 8.04 (b), implies that identifying information be withheld from electronic media UNLESS consent is obtained.

Code 8.04 (c) however, requires obscuring identifying information whenever possible. It is clearly an ethical violation to use client photos on a webpage *without* client consent.

My question is, what about using client photos *if consent has been obtained* to display them on a webpage or in the hallway of an agency?

Is the use of client photos on the web, even with consent for their use, a violation of the BACB Ethics Code?

ETHICS QUESTION #44

I was informed by the principal of a local private school that serves children with special needs that she was presented with an offer by a high-ranking individual from a major southern-city-based behavior analysis company. She stated that this individual offered her an amount of money for each child that she (or anyone else at the school) refers to receive behavioral services from their company in exchange for only allowing this company's therapists into the school.

She stated to me that she was greatly offended by this offer and that she told this person she would in no way tell companies who are helping her other students that they could no longer provide immensely beneficial ABA services to her other students because of this agreement.

Secondary to this offer, the person stated that this agreement is something that has been accepted at other schools.

This tells me that it is possible that a child receiving services with another ABA company cannot be observed or treated for any socially significant behavioral issues or deficits in their school setting by anyone else other than those employed by a particular company.

In turn, when probing for barriers to entering schools to do behavior analysis consulting, my fellow colleagues said they had actually been denied access to other schools and which stated they "couldn't let them in."

In my honest opinion, this raises a massive issue for the ABA community in my state, the field of ABA in general and most importantly, the clients. Not only is this a bribe by this company representative but, this also results in what I believe is possible coercion in the form of telling parents if you want your child's services at the school (which happens often) then you must go to this company or change companies regardless of effectiveness.

What can be done about this?

ETHICS QUESTION #45

I have a colleague who is a BCBA and she is part owner of an ABA service provider company. She does not use her real name on Facebook, but she does list BCBA as her credential and lists her job as manager of the ABA service provider (with the name attached). Yesterday, she responded to another student's Facebook post about an FDA position on vaccines by saying (I'm summarizing) that she believes vaccines cause autism and are a conspiracy by big pharma, so she does not vaccinate her child. She further suggested that the only way to know for sure if vaccines cause autism is for everyone to stop vaccinating for five years to see if overall prevalence rates of autism decrease. I'm concerned that she is advocating her anti-vaccination stance to the families and staff members with whom she works. I'm further concerned because as a colleague, she not only represents the field of applied behavior analysis, but also the educational program where I work. Further, her organization provides a training site for BCBAs coming through the ABA program at my school. If she is advocating this position, she has a wide audience.

My question is: What steps (if any) should I take? Is this a reportable offense? It's likely that if I do report and she loses her license (I don't know if this could happen or is likely), she will also lose her livelihood and she is a new parent. Students at my program will also suffer as they're accruing BCBA hours through her organization. I'm not sure what to do and would appreciate any guidance you can provide.

ETHICS QUESTION #46

Message: I am an RBT. One of my supervisors has a client on her caseload who has engaged in noncompliance/tantrums/aggressions for the past year. These behaviors have increased in frequency and duration. While no formal data is taken, I would estimate that the client now spends 70% of his time at the clinic engaged in problem behavior.

The BCBA *has never conducted a functional analysis* and no formal plan exists to respond to the problem behavior, despite the fact that I have asked for these things multiple times.

There is also no reinforcement system in place to proactively treat the problem behavior. The same demands are placed each day, and the child is expected to comply 100% of the time.

The consequences delivered change almost daily, and often the BCBA or another RBT will physically hold the child in the chair. I refuse to do this.

I have taken this issue to the clinical director, who has agreed with me that it is wrong, but all she has done is agree to observe a session and make suggestions for the BCBA. She has expressed that because it is not her client, she cannot make decisions about the treatment plan.

I feel that this situation is highly unethical in multiple ways.

No assessments have been conducted other than an initial FBA that is a year old (and the child did not engage in noncompliance during the assessment). There is no formal plan to respond to the behavior, nor is any real data being taken and analyzed. I feel that holding the child in the chair is an unsafe consequence that is doing harm to the child. I have gone both to the BCBA and the clinical director, with no actions taken to improve the situation. At this point, I do not know what to do, and I am also afraid that I will lose my job if I report the situation.

This BCBA's behavior is similar with all of her clients. Most of her data sheets are copied and pasted between clients, she does not supervise her RBTs or assess new problem behaviors, and most of her clients make limited progress.

Do you have any advice for me?

ETHICS QUESTION #47

I work for a small private ABA clinic in the southeast that is owned by a person who is trained both as a physical therapist (PT) and an occupational therapist (OT). She owns the ABA company and a separate company (that ABA shares a building with) that provides OT, PT, and speech and language therapy (SLT) services.

Many of the clients seen by the ABA company are also seen by the other clinic as well. The owner also sees clients as an OT or PT (often OT for the ASD kids).

My question/concern is as follows: Last week, a parent of a child I see (as a case supervisor) informed me that the owner, who has been providing OT therapy weekly, recommended a SIT (sensory integration therapy) procedure to manage the child's SIB. The problem is, while we try to help the clients understand that the two companies are distinct entities, many families are understandably unclear on this (given the same owner and office). While I had no issue recommending a behavior analytic intervention for the treatment of the SIB (a successful treatment had been provided several months earlier with resurgence recently occurring), I was left wondering how this is perceived by the client. On the one hand, the OT services are provided at the clinic while the ABA is provided in-home, but as an owner of an ABA program, the owner's recommendations could be fortified by her relation to ABA services.

So, 1) should I bring this concern to the owner and, 2) as the owner of an ABA company, does our field's Code of Ethics apply to her? Is she responsible in an alternative clinical practice setting to adhere to her other company's requirements?

Thank you in advance for your consideration.

ETHICS QUESTION #48

I work for a school district and we are cleaning out our old files. The BCBA team is wondering if there are official guidelines for storing and destroying old data for exited students?

We are curious about:

1. Storage (does it need to be in a locked file in a locked room)?
2. What needs to be in a client file?
3. How long to keep a file?
4. How do you destroy the file?
5. How do we keep e-data secure?

ETHICS QUESTION #49

One of my employees referred her friend's child to me. I was going to accept the case and not have the employee who is a friend on the case. I set up an evaluation and met the family at the house. The mother was very nice. The issue I had is it was difficult to walk up the stairs because of clutter on the stairs. There was long box halfway up the stairs but there was a small path I could maneuver around. There were other things on the stairs as well. I felt some parts of the house were not clean (crumbs next to me on the table in the house, dusty things). The children did NOT appear to be in danger at all from the unkempt house and they were clean. I just knew right away we could not do home-based therapy in the house due to OSHA laws but it made the evaluation a little awkward.

I didn't feel comfortable navigating their house so I mainly observed the three-year-old boy with an ASD diagnosis. Usually if the child feels comfortable, I try to play and interact and have a fun time to make the evaluation exciting. I had the mom sign the consent for the VB Mapp and the structured ABC assessment I was going to do. I explained to her that I was going to mostly observe to figure out why the aggressive behaviors are occurring and to do the VB Mapp assessment. I told the mother to just go about what they normally do. I told her it may be a little awkward but I need a good picture of what is going on. The child I was observing had very flexible spontaneous language so I didn't think that I needed to do a lot of direct testing. I did ask him a few questions and he would politely decline to answer. I didn't want to push him on the first day of meeting him so I didn't ask too many questions. Also, his deficits are not language related; they are in the areas of play skills and social skills so a lot of one-on-one direct testing was not warranted.

I also asked the mom questions from the AFLS home assessment. I learned that the child was aggressing on the family members at a high rate for attention. I am not sure if the mother liked hearing this information from me because she believed that maybe her son didn't realize what he was doing hurts people. She also said that they don't 100% believe the child has autism. I mentioned how autism can be different in each individual. I explained my concern over the boy's leisure and play skills and how children his age usually find things on their own to play with. The mother said that most children his age need a lot of direction on play activities. The mother seems in semi-denial.

I told the mother that due to the boy's aggression, which is mainly targeted at his sister, it may be easier if we do sessions at a preschool or daycare to work on play and social skills. Another option is teaching the sister how to respond differently so as not to reinforce him. At this time, I did not mention the home and the OSHA concerns because the dynamic with the boy and his sister was enough to make me recommend doing therapy outside of the home. Also, the fact that he has social skills deficits warranted another location for therapy with peers. I can do some parent-and-sister training in the home to help decrease the aggression.

I tried to reach out to the mother after the evaluation but she seemed to be avoiding me for the next four days. I needed more intake forms signed and she wouldn't respond. (This was a lesson learned by me; all forms need to be signed prior to the evaluation). The mother finally sent the forms at the end of the week. When I was leaving the house that day, the sister said she thought I would be playing with them. I have a feeling they were not happy with the evaluation because it was mostly observation, but I did the best I could with the condition of the home, the dynamics of the family, and the boy's attention-seeking aggression. I did my best to describe what I was going to do and my recommendations.

Mom said she was looking into the local school district as another option so I said to let me know what she thought about the district and to let me know if she would be sending him there rather than working with me. I said I would be happy to do some home parent training if they decide to go with the school system.

I guess I am asking, do I even mention the OSHA laws I need to follow? I am usually okay with giving feedback but I wouldn't want to insult someone the first time I met them.

ETHICS QUESTION #50

I live in Dubai and I have been a behavioral therapist since 2011. I am an RBT and I have started my BCBA course, in which I am learning about Ethics in Applied Behavior Analysis. As I read through the core principles of Ethics, I can see that my supervisor doesn't follow the Ethics Code. I believe I should report some of the issues below.

Specifically, I provide home-based services and I often see my clients getting slapped in the face by their parents. In fact, one day when I went for the session, my six-year-old client pointed to the marks on his face and reported that his mother hit him. When I confronted the mother, she immediately confessed saying that she is fed up with the child not listening to her. I discussed the entire situation with my supervisor who didn't seem to be taking any action. When the parents came for the review session with my supervisor, the mother slapped the child in front of my supervisor, and the child yelled and jumped from his chair. My supervisor did not bother to look into this.

I have emails to document that I also reported to my supervisors another client who is 11-years old and both of her parents hit her frequently. She sometimes screams during our sessions, "I DONT WANT TO GO TO CORNER." Her mother reported to me proudly, "I gave her a slap because she passed urine in her bed." All of this was reported to my supervisor via my emails and she did not bother to take any action.

It became very difficult to help the child as her problem behaviors were increasing during the sessions. She would scream and would be extremely afraid if her mother came close to her. With no help provided by the supervisor for this particular case, I had to refer the client to my supervisor.

When my clients are engaging in disruptive behaviors, I often ask my supervisor to help me with a plan to help the child, but there is no response. She expects us to come up with our own consequences and is not even bothered by the problems. She says that we all manage disruptive behaviors which is right on her part but I am an RBT who should be given guidelines by a BCBA as to how to change the child's behavior.

Parents often express their distress to me that my supervisor is not cooperative, she does not arrange a review meeting to discuss the child's progress, and she is not sending the latest program for working with the child.

The centers providing ABA services are not as large as they are in the United States so clients have to depend on services that are available.

ETHICS QUESTION #51

I recently gave a 30-day written notice to my employer due to unethical practices. I felt I could no longer continue to work for an unethical company. The company rejected my 30-days-notice, and instead gave me 10 minutes to pack up my belongings and leave the facility.

All of my supporting documents of fraudulent paperwork is with my supervisors and the facility and I have no further access to this documentation.

Although I have documented several ethical code violations in my own record of dates and by whom, I do not have the actual documents to support my claims. Will the BACB look at my case even though I don't have the original documents to support these claims?

ETHICS QUESTION #52

If an RBT is listing herself as a "behavior analyst" on social media (e.g. Facebook and LinkedIn), it seems that this violates Code 10.07. I have notified this RBT (who reports that she will take the BCBA exam the next time it is scheduled) that this label should be changed on her social media and anywhere else.

This RBT was also involved in a recent situation in which I reported a BCBA who provided a falsified 40-hour RBT Course certificate and falsified the completion of an RBT Competency Assessment.

In that case, I reported the BCBA to the BACB, but didn't report the applicant.

I instead provided education and feedback to the applicant. That applicant is now an RBT under yet another BCBA. (1) If this now registered RBT responds to me and changes her status, do I still need to report her to the BACB? (2) If she does not respond to me and does not change her status, should I contact her current BCBA supervisor or file a report with the BCBA or both?

ETHICS QUESTION #53

I am a BCBA. I am also a mother to a child with an ASD diagnosis. My son is doing amazingly well on his training programs (he had received 25–40 hours per week of ABA from the age of 2–6 and had mastered out of all areas of the VB-MAPP except social a few years ago). Basically, his biggest impairments are his social skills, and executive functioning skills; he has some fine-motor delays, and speech/articulation issues for which he sees a speech therapist. He does not engage in challenging behaviors (aggression, SIB, etc.) and he is a very well behaved, and respectful child.

Because I want to be his mom, not his BCBA, I recently sought out ABA services from XYZ Company for the purposes of working on his social/executive functioning deficits, and to provide school consultation and observations. His school will not let me observe him because I am his mother, but will allow a hired BCBA to come in to observe and offer recommendations. To clarify; he isn't having significant behavior challenges at school, but some minor noncompliance that I believe is being reinforced by the paraprofessional working with him. I hoped that if we got a BCBA, the BCBA would be able to observe and make sure the school paraprofessional is fading prompts, and challenging him enough.

My ethics concern is regarding the BCBA from XYZ Company that was assigned to us. I will try to explain as well as I can below:

1. First, the BCBA that was assigned to us is new and just passed her exam a few months ago. This BCBA came to my home for the intake interview and she had her supervisor on her iPad (on FaceTime or Skype) because she is not yet credentialed with insurance. The BCBA that was on Skype did not say a word the entire time, and it appeared as if he wasn't even paying attention to our conversation and was only there for the purpose of billing. This felt wrong to me, but I am not sure if it violates any ethical guidelines.

2. Second, the BCBA that came to my home did not spend any time with my son (except for a few minutes when she arrived and said hello to him). She relied solely on the parent questionnaire on the XYZ Company Portal, and questions during the intake interview to develop his treatment plan. She did not do any direct assessment, data collection, or observation of him. During this intake, I did inform her that I am also a BCBA. We discussed XYZ's new arrival in my town as a satellite office that does only in-home services (with an actual clinic in the nearby city). The BCBA informed me that they are planning to open a clinic as soon as they have enough clients. She stated that my son was one of the last ones she needed in order to have enough to open their clinic. About two weeks later, the BCBA informed me that she had gotten an authorization from my insurance company and returned to my home to review his treatment plan (this was three days ago).

3. The BCBA informed me that she had requested, and been approved for 25 hours/week in his authorization from my insurance company. I was very surprised by this, and had asked her why she had asked for 25 hours per week. She stated that she based this on when we were available, and how many hours my child could get in during that time. The schedule she planned for my son was that since he would be at school from 8:50am–3:30pm M–F (we get home at 3:45), that she would like to have a therapist come to our home M–F from 4 or 4:30 until 8pm, and on Saturdays to have two sessions back to back with two different therapists. This was highly concerning to me, and throughout the conversation, she was entirely focused on him getting the full 25 hours a week. She again mentioned that they now have enough clients to open a clinic, and that she believes it will be done by December. (I feel that it is important here to contrast that my professional opinion, as a BCBA, would be to provide my son with a Focused ABA program, and that two to three afternoon sessions per week would be an appropriate amount of services for his level of need and deficits.)

4. My feeling here is that the BCBA is simply trying to meet her quota. Once she has so many hours/clients, they can then open the clinic. I felt that this was more of her agenda than providing appropriate ABA to my son.

5. I informed the BCBA that I feel that the number of hours that she has recommended was too many, I did not feel that would be appropriate for him, and that I feel it is much too high for a highly functioning kid with his skillset. She gave me a guilt trip and informed me that research shows that less than 25 hours a week is not as effective, and she continued to try and convince me to schedule him for 25 hours. I informed her that I did not feel it is appropriate for my child to not have any free-time during his weekdays, and that it seems inappropriate to schedule any kid for every free moment that they have during the week. I clarified with her that what she was recommending, which was to barely have any down-time, and then be in therapy from 4–8pm, then go to bed at 8:30. I explained that this doesn't allow for family time, or play time with his siblings, etc. I was significantly concerned over her recommendation and the pressure she was placing on me as a parent (and fellow BCBA). I mainly am concerned for parents that do not know better and are pressured to accept this highly inappropriate schedule because of her misquoted data regarding ABA not being effective if it is under 25 hours/week.

6. I also responded to her pressure by saying that I can understand her recommending 25 hours/week if he needed a comprehensive ABA program, if he had significant behavior challenges, high levels of skill deficits, or if he hadn't had years of ABA already, and I re-informed her that he has already done that with his

40 hours a week of Comprehensive ABA between the ages of 2–6, and I was seeking a Focused ABA program for his social skills and executive functioning skills only. She looked confused and changed the topic leaving me to believe that she does not know the difference between Focused ABA and Comprehensive ABA. This also was highly concerning to me that she is not familiar with the Practice Guidelines the BACB established.

7. In addition, the treatment plan goals that she had selected for my son were not appropriate. She selected skills that he had mastered four years ago, and when I informed her that he already does that, she would say something along the lines of "well, we will just start with these skills and then master them out, and move on from there." Instead of assessing him properly, or collecting baseline data on her target skills (for acquisition), it feels like she was just guessing and there was no data behind the targets that were selected. She even had chosen noncompliance as a target, even though I had informed her that he is very compliant and that we do not have behavior challenges at home.

8. The BCBA also told me that she would need to do two to three hours of parent training with me each month. I asked her if this is an insurance requirement, or if it is from XYZ Company. She told me it is from XYZ Company. I said I understand the importance of parent training, but I am a BCBA, and feel that it is not necessary to train me on ABA techniques to use with my son; yet she insisted that it was required. I do not feel that this is right for her to have three more billable hours per month to train me on things I already know how to do. It just seems wrong to me.

9. Lastly, I had asked her if they use the AFLS, and named some other protocols, and she said, no, that they use their own (that XYZ Company had developed), and this also felt wrong to me. I feel that whatever protocols are most applicable to a client should be used, and not just the one that the company developed. For example, I use the ABLLS-R on certain clients, and the VB-MAPP on others depending on which is more appropriate for that particular client.

I apologize for the length of this email. What I really am trying to find out is what do I do from here? I know that as a BCBA, I am supposed to go directly to the individual (BCBA), bring it to her attention and try to resolve the matter prior to reporting to the BACB. I feel comfortable doing this, but I don't know if I am supposed to act as a BCBA, or as a concerned parent that feels like a BCBA is trying to take advantage of getting the most billable hours possible to meet her quota.

In addition, I want to express that I feel that this is a huge problem that I have observed over the years where BCBAs become certified, and do not really know what they are doing. My experience this week was truly similar to those I have read about on some parent support groups (and I had thought were exaggerated, or made up) where parents express their dissatisfaction with ABA/BCBA's. This BCBA really was just like a robot in an ABA factory trying to meet quotas on billable hours and not really considering the actual needs of the client, or using data to make decisions as to what would be best for this client as an individual, and as a human being, and not just as a tool for billing 25 hours per week.

Can you give me some direction from here? How should I address this?

ETHICS QUESTION #54

I am writing about an ethical issue that has come to my attention since relocating and joining a new company. I appreciate any guidance you may be able to provide.

As I have started taking over cases at my new company I have come across an issue that pertains to use and dissemination of Intellectual Property.

The prior BCBA (whose cases I am taking over) has completed a variety of assessments including the ABLLS-R, VB-MAPP and Essentials for Living with clients. During the transition, she provided electronic copies of the scoring grids but not the protocol books for the clients. I emailed a request to the BCBA requesting the protocol books, but she did not respond.

I reached out to the company owner (my supervisor) as I have a client who is in need of an assessment. Her initial response via email was, "I have blank protocols. You can make copies and use what you need."

As this is inappropriate (in my understanding of Intellectual Property and copyright laws), I responded with, "It is my understanding that since these are copyrighted materials they are not licensed for duplication. Is that correct? If you have a different understanding or agreement with the developer(s), I would be very interested in learning more. Otherwise, if we don't want to deal with those complications, can we brainstorm other solutions to accessing the needed assessments?"

My goal essentially was to bring to her attention the issues of copying copyrighted material and to identify solutions—either purchase the protocols appropriately or to identify/develop assessment strategies that do not involve copyrighted material. She responded by saying we would talk about it in person when we met. During that meeting, she shared the VB-MAPP Guidebook, but said she would have to get the protocol from home. I said this would be fine because we had a staff meeting coming up and I could get it then.

After this meeting, I reached out to the publisher of the VB-MAPP regarding appropriate usage as I wanted to make sure I was correct in my understanding prior to making any statements/additional requests for individual protocols. He was very helpful in clarifying my presented questions. From those email conversations, he confirmed my statement that making copies of protocol books was inappropriate and he addressed some other usage concerns including the Excel grid and a violation of the BACB Ethics Code if the person involved is a behavior analyst.

My company met this morning in a staff meeting. Three BCBAs—including myself were present along with four RBTs. At the end of the meeting, my supervisor presented me with a protocol book for my client. She stated that if I "needed" each client to have their own protocol she would likely purchase the application rather than books. I said I appreciated that and would be happy to work with either the book or application, whichever the company felt was most appropriate. She then went on to say that the company did not typically purchase a protocol for each student. I stated that I would be more comfortable since the cases would be under my certification if each child had his or her own protocol as it was an issue of Intellectual Property and making copies is not permitted. Her response was "yes, technically it is, but" and turned to a newly hired RBT in the meeting and asked if they (her former company) provided a protocol book for each child to which the RBT responded "no." I also mentioned that should an issue arise from a family against the company, that a copied assessment would not be considered an appropriate diagnostic tool for services in court (based on my conversations with the publisher). She agreed but said it would be unlikely to happen. I agreed that while unlikely, it would still be in the company's best interest to have individualized protocols for each client. I followed up with it also being a part of our Ethical Code. Again, she responded "yes, technically but" and followed with a rough timeframe of it being 20 years that she has been working in this manner with no negative consequences. The RBT that she had turned to previously then also stated, "yeah, but the code changes all the time." I was a bit in shock by the blatant disregard for the code and the conversation ended with that. I thanked her for the protocol book and wished everyone a good day since the meeting was over.

My questions/comments are as follows:

1. Based on the information collected from the publisher contact and in review of the BACB Professional and Ethical Compliance Code, it appears as if there is a violation.

   a. Specifically, it appears that the owner is practicing unethically by photocopying copyright protocols and encouraging staff to (8.02 (a)).
   b. Additionally, there may be grounds for 2.10—Documenting Professional Work and Research, as a new BCBA to the case is unable to transition services smoothly due to the lack of documentation of the assessment; and 2.11—Records and Data as the prior assessments were not "maintained, and stored" appropriately.

      Would this be more of an issue with the BCBA who transitioned off the cases, the owner, or both?

2. Regarding the steps to addressing an alleged violation, it is my understanding that the first step is to discuss the concern with the person committing the violation and try to correct for it. I feel I have done this with the owner of the company through the email conversations as well as the discussion in the meeting. These did not in result what I would consider "resolved" outcomes. While she is willing to purchase protocol books for me, the owner's overall approach still seems to be making copies and supporting that decision in front of her staff.

3. Additionally, I am disappointed that despite knowing that it is inappropriate to copy these materials, the owner is advocating that we do so in front of the staff. It is also unfortunate that this is the model being set forth for those she is supervising RBT's and those seeking certification as a BCBA. This is possibly a violation of 6.0—Responsibility to the Profession of Behavior Analysis, and possibly 5.0—Supervision or 10.05—Compliance with Supervision.

4. Based on the information provided, do you think this would warrant a filing of a complaint with the BACB? At this point, and based on the owner's comments during this morning's meeting, I am planning on doing so for the owner. I would appreciate more clarification on the role of the BCBA who transferred her cases to me—perhaps she asked and the owner told her to copy protocols so she was following company directives?

   a. If there are any other remedial steps between those that I have taken (discussing it directly with the owner, bringing the Code to her attention) prior to filing a complaint, I would like to take that first.

   b. If there are any steps I should take with the BCBA who transitioned off the cases, I would appreciate guidance to that as well.

5. Following the staff meeting this morning, I am left with the feeling that the culture set forth by this business is one that is not as committed to upholding the ethical practices our field strives for and despite the attempted resolution, is unlikely to make a significant change in practices. As such, I feel I must separate myself from this business and resign. This is very unfortunate since I recently relocated about 900 miles to take this position. Would it be appropriate to professionally address my reason for leaving being the ethical concerns I have? Also, if I file a complaint, should I notify the owner?

6. I only started a few months ago so it will be a quick departure, but I think it would be in my and the client's best interest for me to resign now, rather than wait months to avoid interrupting or discontinuing services. I plan to offer four weeks to support a transition plan. I only work part-time for the company, so I feel that this is an appropriate length of time.

ETHICS QUESTION #55

I have a few questions.

1. I got assigned a new BCBA supervisor about three months ago. We met the week she started and went over the supervision contract that my old BCBA and I drew up. The new supervisor also had the sample contract that the board provides. She said she would make some changes and adjust it to fit our needs and get it back to me to sign. I just realized when organizing my supervision pages that she never did get a contract back to me to sign. This means we have no supervision contract and haven't had one for the last three months.

   I am an RBT but currently in my third class for my BCaBA so I am following those experience standards. Do my hours from the last three months not count? Is she at fault for this? I think she is at fault for sure. According to the BACB Experience Standards:

   "DOCUMENTATION OF ONGOING SUPERVISION: The supervisee and supervisor are responsible for collecting documentation on the Experience Supervision Form during each supervisory period. One form should be completed within each supervisory period, ideally at each meeting. Backdated forms will not be accepted. The BACB reserves the right to request this documentation at any time following an individual's application to take the certification exam. This documentation should NOT be submitted with an exam application unless specifically requested by the BACB."

2. There is a BCBA who no longer works at our company. A new BCBA took over her caseload. I have been expected to work with clients that still have old behavior reduction plans. The oldest plan goes back nine months.

   a. Can we implement plans written by a BCBA who no longer works for us? I am guessing probably not because these plans don't include the current diagnosis of ASD and are not current on behavior.

      How long does a behavior reduction plan usually last or for how long is it valid?

   b. For some of the clients I have been providing services for, the BCBA just met the parents since getting switched to these clients almost two months ago. Is this unethical?

   c. I have also been told to use interventions without signed consent of new goals that are not even listed in the original plans from the previous BCBA.

      Is this a fault of my own or the new BCBA? Is a transition period, acceptable? If yes, about how long?

      My goal here is not to get anyone in trouble. I just want to learn what is ethical and unethical before I approach my superiors about the issues I am experiencing.

2

Response from the Ethicist

ETHICS QUESTION #1—RESPONSE FROM THE ETHICIST

It was brought to my attention that one of my RBTs has a picture of an old client (i.e. no longer receiving services from us) on her phone. The mother of the client sent the picture to the RBT and frequently gives us updates on the child's well-being due to the family moving from one state to another. Is this a violation of Code 2.06 (e)?

> **No, having a photo of a former client and keeping in touch with a that individual does not break confidentiality since they do not have a formal therapist/client relationship.**

I'm assuming this is not a problem since the child is no longer a client; however, I know one ethical code item states waiting two years before having contact with a family who was once in a professional relationship with you (Code 1.07 (b, c) Exploitative Relationships). Yet, this Code states "sexual relationships" which is definitely not occurring.

> **This is correct. The two years is intended for situations where a behavior analyst became romantically attracted to a client (usually a male BCBA and a single mom of a client). Your RBT's situation does not violate the Code.**

The key words in 2.06 (e) are "current clients."[1] Behavior analysts work very closely with their clients and gain a great deal of private information that should not be shared with anyone outside of the behavior analysis treatment team. Once that client has graduated or moved on as in this case, the RBT or other behavior analyst may keep in touch with that client but the private information about them must be kept confidential.

ETHICS QUESTION #2—RESPONSE FROM THE ETHICIST

My question is whether a behavior analyst may do a presentation for an advocacy group or a local parent support group for parents of children with some form of disability.

Presenting to groups is actually encouraged in Code 6.02.

6.02 Disseminating Behavior Analysis ^{RBT}
Behavior analysts promote behavior analysis by making information about it available to the public through presentations, discussions, and other media.

In most cases, one can assume that presenting to a parent group is a problem because parents are "potential users of services who, because of their particular circumstances, are vulnerable to undue influence." I just wanted some clarification.

We want behavior analysts to make our applied science available to the public, and speaking to groups like this is not a form of solicitation (see Code 8.06) since it is *invited*. Considering the group nature of the presentation, these parents are *not vulnerable*. Reaching out to the public helps our field by presenting basic concepts of behavior analysis in a way that allows the audience to understand how we think about behavior and our standards of service. Behavior analysts can discuss Best Practices and our Code of Ethics so that those in attendance will become discriminating consumers going forward. What is discouraged is business solicitation in the disguise of education; we are not selling time-shares or promoting Alaskan cruises. To invite parents to come to an educational talk and then go into a sales pitch is a bad (and unethical) plan that would most likely backfire. The word would get around that behavior analysts are just trying to drum up business with these presentations.

One other caution is that the content of the talk should not be such that it encourages attendees to think that they can walk out of the meeting and start using behavior analysis principles with difficult or dangerous behaviors without some assistance from a BCBA. They *can* be encouraged to use prompts and reinforcement to increase a desired behavior and to ignore minor misbehavior while reinforcing following requests or incompatible behavior. Beyond that, there is some risk that some members of the audience may think they can take on severe behavior problems. A good thrust for a general talk is to promote primary prevention of behavior problems through the use of NCR and DRA.

Educating the public about behavior analysis is one of the most important activities for behavior analysts. We have some history to overcome ("You're making children into robots . . . ") and we need to let consumers know about our basic values and our modern methods. We can tell them that we are interested in the "causes" of behavior problems (functional analysis, MOs) and describe the limiting conditions of our concept of evidence-based treatments and best practices. Finally, we can translate some of our Code of Ethics into plain English so they understand why we operate as we do ("Consent of parents is essential to everything we do . . . ").

ETHICS QUESTION #3—RESPONSE FROM THE ETHICIST

I have a quick ethics question. I know that as BCBAs we do not solicit testimonials but is it acceptable to approach a student from the classroom in which I am already working?

> **Probably not since this would be an in-person solicitation which is not allowed under 8.06 of the Code of Ethics.**
>
> ### 8.06 In-Person Solicitation [RBT]
> *Behavior analysts do not engage, directly or through agents, in uninvited in-person solicitation of business from actual or potential users of services who, because of their particular circumstances, are vulnerable to undue influence. Organizational behavior management or performance management services may be marketed to corporate entities regardless of their projected financial position.*

I work with a client in a classroom in a school for children with disabilities. There is a peer that I feel could benefit greatly from my services. In the classroom, I have successfully paired him as a peer for my client and have even helped him acquire the beginnings of functional communication in order to facilitate interactions with my client. I would like to offer my services to his mother but I feel like that might not be allowed.

> **Correct, this would not be allowed as described above.**

I cannot reason why but it feels like I shouldn't be singling him out of a classroom of children.

> **The reason is that this would be a type of exploitation (see Code 1.07) where you, as an authority in the school, are soliciting business from a family. The family would be in an awkward position and would have a hard time saying no if they did not want your services.**
>
> ### 1.07 Exploitative Relationships [RBT]
> (a) *Behavior analysts do not exploit persons over whom they have supervisory, evaluative, or other authority such as students, supervisees, employees, research participants, and clients.*

What do you think?

> **If you have permission to work with this child as a "peer therapist" for your client, then you may continue. At some point, the parents may think of asking you for additional services, but the request needs to come from the parents with no prompting from you.**

In-person solicitation is typically thought of as "ambulance chasing" where a provider comes across a person in distress and offers her services. The person, under stress of some sort, and anxious for some quick relief or at least assurances says, "Yes, sure sign me up . . . " and then later realizes that they really do not need the assistance after all but feel caught because they signed a contract. In this case, the behavior analyst should not approach the parents of the child that is serving as the "peer therapist" because the behavior analyst would be taking advantage of her position of authority in the classroom. This would be a subtle case of exploitation which is not permitted under our Code.

ETHICS QUESTION #4—RESPONSE FROM THE ETHICIST

I have an ethics question. I have been at several IEP meetings where a particular individual is using the title of Behavior Analyst when introducing herself to parents, district representatives, and whoever else is in attendance. This individual is currently collecting her practicum hours and has not yet sat for the exam. I believe she is at 500 hours.

Do you have first-hand knowledge of this information?

When questioned as to why this individual is representing herself as a Behavior Analyst, her district is saying that is okay for her to do so because she is in the process of becoming a Behavior Analyst and that is the job title for which she was hired.

Is she an RBT or BCaBA?

Is it ethical for this person to be calling herself a Behavior Analyst?

No, this is a violation of 10.07 of the Code of Ethics:

10.07 Discouraging Misrepresentation by Non-Certified Individuals[RBT]
Behavior analysts report non-certified (and, if applicable, non-registered) practitioners to the appropriate state licensing board and to the BACB if the practitioners are misrepresenting BACB certification or registration status.

Also, if you look at the definition of "Behavior Analyst" in the Glossary of the Code you will find:

"Behavior Analyst"
Behavior analyst refers to an individual who holds the BCBA or BCaBA credential, an individual authorized by the BACB to provide supervision, or a coordinator of a BACB Approved Course Sequences. Where Code elements are deemed relevant to the practice of an RBT, the term "behavior analyst" includes the behavior technician.

You could bring this directly to the attention of the person rather than the district and point out the two items above. If she does not respond, then you could bring it to the attention of her supervisor.

This is not an uncommon event in our field. Many organizations do not understand the difference between a job title and a professional certification. For example, a person with little to no expertise in behavior analysis might have the job title of behavior technician or behavior specialist. There could even be a job title: Behavior Analyst, which would really confuse the public. We much prefer the use of the BACB designations since they clearly delineate the difference between high school (RBT), undergraduate degree (BCaBA), master's (BCBA), and doctoral level (BCBA-D). An RBT who is studying to become a BCBA is still an RBT; RBTs cannot call themselves Behavior Analysts until they have taken all the courses, completed their supervision, and passed the exam.

ETHICS QUESTION #5—RESPONSE FROM THE ETHICIST

Dear Behavior Analysis Ethicist,

Thank you for taking the time to read this! I am concerned that I am working for a company that is unethical in its practices, and I am unsure of how to proceed. Some background: I am currently employed as a BCBA by an ABA company that is owned by a pediatric neurologist. Management is pressuring me to implement procedures written by the neurologist that advocate a procedure called "quiet sitting" which requires a child be kept sitting and engaged in absolutely nothing for ten-minute intervals. It does not teach replacement behaviors and the procedure is missing several components of an ethical behavior program.

The clinical director (also a BCBA) is directing me to implement the methods from the book in my ABA programs along with programs that are outside of my scope of practice (OT, speech, academic programs).

Do you have this in writing from the clinical director? The clinical director is actually the one who is out of bounds here. Take a look at 1.02 (a).

Do you have this in writing?

When I informed management that this is not within my field's Code of Ethics,

I was told that I had a narrow-minded interpretation of my ethical code and it may cause me to lose my job.

No, you are correct.

I found out that children are being restrained during ABA programs that include "quiet sitting."

I am unsure if it is best for me to move on to another company or if there is more I should do to advocate for these recipients as well as ABA as a whole. Do you have any suggestions to ensure that I meet my ethical obligations?

Do the parents know about this?

It is unlikely that you are going to be successful in changing the orientation of this organization, but you at least need to inform the BCBA clinical director of your concerns under 7.02 (c) of the Code of Ethics. Then, take the necessary steps if you do not get an appropriate response, including giving 30-days-notice and finding another job where you will be safe in operating within the bounds of our Code of Ethics.

It is very difficult to have an influence as a behavior analyst in an organization that has a completely different theoretical orientation from behavior analysis. It would be even more difficult to have an influence when the organization's non-behavioral work has been developed by faculty at a well-known university as is the case here. New students looking for their first jobs should be aware that there are a large number of organizations that nod to behavior analysis, use selected portions of our technology, and bill for ABA services, but do not have the same commitment to behavior analysis as a separate, evidence-based approach. If you remain within your boundaries of competence as a Board Certified Behavior Analyst and work for a company that respects those boundaries, you should flourish as a professional.

ETHICS QUESTION #6—RESPONSE FROM THE ETHICIST

Good evening,

I am an ABA graduate student coming to the end of my degree. As a part of our course we complete a functional analysis within our supervision setting.

As a graduate student studying ABA, you are under the Code of Ethics.

I am also a foster parent. My six-year-old foster daughter who has autism has begun engaging in some worrying behavior at school and at home. I'd like to conduct a functional analysis on the behavior with the support of some fellow students. However, the state has legal custody of her, and I am paid by the state to care for her. What are my ethical concerns here?

You would need written consent from the agency that has legal custody of the child under 3.03 of the Code of Ethics. But, since she is your foster daughter, this would constitute a multiple-relationship, with respect to the child and is covered under 1.06:

1.06 Multiple Relationships and Conflicts of Interest[RBT]
1.06 (a) *Due to the potentially harmful effects of multiple relationships, behavior analysts avoid multiple relationships.*
  (b) *Behavior analysts must always be sensitive to the potentially harmful effects of multiple relationships. If behavior analysts find that, due to unforeseen factors, a multiple relationship has arisen, they seek to resolve it.*
  (c) *Behavior analysts recognize and inform clients and supervisees about the potential harmful effects of multiple relationships.*

Are they insurmountable?

The ethical concerns here prevent you from treating your own daughter. Even if you adopted this child, you would still have the multiple relationship problem. You should seek the assistance of a BCBA unrelated to you to do the assessment. If this works, you will no doubt be trained by that BCBA to implement a BIP for your (foster) daughter.

Dealing with multiple relationships is one of the most common problems that behavior analysts will encounter. A behavior analyst is asked to supervise an RBT who is their cousin; or the son of the CEO wants a placement at the facility so he can get his supervision hours. Or a BCBA may develop a romantic relationship with a member of her team. The variations appear endless. Can an owner who is a BCBA hire her daughter who is working on her RBT or BCBA supervision hours? No. Can a parent join the Board of directors of the private school where her son receives ABA services? No. Can an office manager who just discovered that her son has been diagnosed with ASD bring him to the agency where she works and enroll him for behavior analysis treatment? No. All of these situations represent dual-role relationships and are not allowed by the Code of Ethics 1.06. Here's the dynamic: There is a conflict of interest or *perceived* conflict of interest that always occurs when a child's parent works at the agency where they are treated: 1) other parents will likely feel that their child is receiving lesser services because an employee's child is receiving more treatment or higher quality services or perhaps exempt from the regular rules as established by treatment teams; 2) as an employee the parent of a child enrolled at the agency will have access to confidential information about all the other clients, which probably violates HIPAA; 3) when behavioral staff are meeting with the parents to discuss treatment issues and options, they will always be aware that they are speaking with a fellow employee; and 4) finally, if for some reason the agency decided to discontinue services for the client under 2.15 of the Code, they would know full well that this could affect the employment of the parent, and vice versa. If they wished to fire the employee/parent, they would be very aware that this would affect the client services for the client.

ETHICS QUESTION #7—RESPONSE FROM THE ETHICIST

I have a concern about a possible ethical violation. I wanted to find out if indeed there has been a violation and what, if anything, I can do about it. I am a BCBA working at an ABA agency. I recently put in my 30-days-notice of resignation, so that I would ideally have enough time to properly transition my cases to another supervisor and say goodbye to my families.

Good, 30-days-notice is the standard.

I was called into a last-minute meeting this morning by our executive director, and she handed me my last paycheck and told me that I was to leave the company effective immediately. I was told that I would not be allowed to properly transition my cases to a new supervisor, and I was not allowed to contact any of my families or staff. I had to hand over all documents then and there, and was told to delete all client contact information from my phone. When I asked them why they were doing this, they would not give me a reason. I asked if I had done anything wrong, and they said no.

I told them I felt this was unethical because it seems like client abandonment. I should also note that several BCBAs have put in their resignation recently, and many others are in the process of interviewing elsewhere so there really isn't anyone available to take my clients right now.

This could very well be the case but it would be now up to the clients themselves who would have to report the ED (if she is a behavior analyst) for *abandonment*.

I am very much concerned for the well-being of my clients and staff, and I do not agree with or feel good about this decision. I feel like this is client abandonment, that I will be leaving staff with no notice or support.

This is unfortunate that this has happened to you but you are not alone. Time and time again, when ethical behavior analysts put in their notice they are almost immediately let go (the company doesn't want you to stay for 20 days for fear that you might negatively influence other staff).

2.15 Interrupting or Discontinuing Services
(e) *Behavior analysts do not abandon clients and supervisees. Prior to discontinuation, for whatever reason, behavior analysts: discuss service needs, provide appropriate pre-termination services, suggest alternative service providers as appropriate, and, upon consent, take other reasonable steps to facilitate timely transfer of responsibility to another provider.*

In this situation, was there an ethical violation and is there anything I can do about it?

Sadly, you really cannot do anything about this unless some of the former clients (parents) contact you. If the clients contact you (you should not contact them), you can inform them of the ethics violation regarding abandonment and tell them how they can file a notice. Other than that, there is nothing else you can do at this point.

##

Two weeks later . . .

I have a question regarding some new developments in my situation. I had a parent (former client) call me today and leave a voicemail saying there's been no supervision for the past three weeks. The parent said the therapists are showing up late and leaving early and there is no one to hold them accountable.

I returned the parent's call to let her know I no longer worked for the company, and I told her to contact the office about it. She said she tried calling the office to ask about a supervisor, and the person she spoke to was very rude. The parent was told that no one was available in that area to supervise and that the therapists will continue going out with no supervision. The parent also said that no one called to tell her about my involuntary termination.

Not surprising.

I am still concerned that this is a case of client abandonment. Should I email the executive director to let her know this parent called me, tell her I feel she is in violation of the Ethics Code, and ask her to resolve the issue?

> **No, you should not contact the ED. Because the information is second-hand to you, the person to report the situation is the parent. The parent should try to meet with the executive director in person and if she is not satisfied, you could remind her that she could file a Notice of Alleged Violation with the BACB.**

I honestly am at a point where I need to let go and move on with my life, but I also don't feel good about just sitting around and doing nothing. Would I be in violation of the Code of Ethics if I don't say something about a violation that I am aware of?

> **This is clearly uncomfortable for you and it is understandable that you feel a need to do something. However, at this point remember, you only have hearsay about what is going on at your former agency and you cannot operate without first-hand information.**

Our Code is clear, "Behavior analysts do not abandon clients . . . " and yet the decision to discharge a client is not usually one that is in the hands of the individual behavior analyst. Further, the term "abandonment" is not used in the Code nor is it defined in the Glossary. "Discontinuation" carries a similar meaning but is also not defined. Behavior analysts become attached to their clients and want to watch out for the best interests of their client until the very last minute and beyond. When most behavior analysts leave a company, they want to transition clients to another competent and caring behavior analyst. Sometimes, the business orientation of these organizations simply does not permit this. This is certainly frustrating to the ethical behavior analyst who understands the real cost of disrupted services to clients cannot be calculated.

ETHICS QUESTION #8—RESPONSE FROM THE ETHICIST

I have a 20-year-old client diagnosed with ASD living in a residential setting, I have a behavior plan in place for his SIB, providing replacement behaviors for the SIB and dealing with his whining. When he doesn't get his way or if a promised reinforcer is not delivered quickly enough, he will whine persistently and can become aggressive. He is about to undergo various treatments for suspected Lyme Disease, Candida infestation, etc. and the interventions are expected to have impact on MOs and SDs.

The parents have sought out a naturopath for the treatment of the yeast infection without consulting the behavior team. I am unable to work directly with the naturopath because he doesn't want to collaborate and the parents are okay with this.

> **This does not sound good. Using a "naturopath" is a questionable treatment mode and under 3.02 of the Code you should suggest that the family seek an actual medical consultation.**

> *3.02 Medical Consultation*
> *Behavior analysts recommend seeking a medical consultation if there is any reasonable possibility that a referred behavior is influenced by medical or biological variables.*

I'm trying to find a comfortable way to look at this but so far, I haven't landed anywhere.

> **Since it appears the family is choosing to take another route for treatment, it would make sense for you to tell the parents behavioral services will be put on hold and they can contact you when the "naturopath" has completed his work. You could explain it will be impossible to evaluate the effects of your program when there are multiple approaches in place.**

I'm told that the expected impact of being Candida free is that behavior is likely to change. Specifically, that if there is no more problem behavior it'll be because of the Candida removal. But if there still is problem behavior, there is probably still Candida. And, of course, they're expecting discomfort in the Candida "removal process."

This is a no-win situation for ABA.

> **Here is what the Mayo Clinic says about Candida:**
> **www.mayoclinic.org/healthy-lifestyle/consumer-health/expert-answers/candida-cleanse/faq-20058174**

After reviewing the state of the science on these things and asking for the naturopath to add any more info and getting no reply, I am at a bit of a loss. It feels like possible crossroads in treatment planning and implementation on the horizon.

> **As above, take a leave of absence until the disease has run its course, but note that the very legitimate Mayo Clinic has a different interpretation of the cause-effect here.**

Since this is an adult and the funds are public, there is no real limit as it's one of the "special circumstances" cases meaning that the money is going to flow and they could probably do dolphin therapy if they wanted and get it paid for.

However, I am wondering where things like substitute decision-maker status of guardian would come into question if the treatments are not evidence-based. And whether I would say that and how.

> **This is clearly a medical issue, and the best thing is to try and educate the parents about what actual medical experts (not naturopaths) think is going on here as per Code 3.02 cited above.**

Thank you for any ideas you may have.

The main problem of your staying in treatment mode while this is going on is that you will have a very difficult time determining what the controlling variables are. You are required by our Code of Ethics to provide evidence-based treatments, which you cannot do under the circumstances.

Two weeks later from the behavior analyst . . .

When I realized that the naturopathic intervention would likely affect the behavior of my client and would not allow me to determine if my behavioral treatment was working I tried to reason with the parents; when they refused I decided to withdraw from the case.

I saw in the ASD Guidelines (p. 40) that Discharge planning was allowed when, "The family and provider are not able to reconcile important issues in treatment planning and delivery" (BACB ASD Guidelines, 2014) and this was my rationale.

Behavior analysts need to be sensitive to the fact that very often there is some medical involvement with a behavior they are treating. The usual situation is that the behavior analyst recommends a medical consultation as an alternative to a behavioral treatment as in the case of head banging or food refusal. In this unusual case, the parents appear set on using an alternative treatment and are not interested, which is their choice, but this alternative treatment will likely interfere with the behavioral prescription so backing away until the naturopath's work is completed is probably the best course of action.

ETHICS QUESTION #9—RESPONSE FROM THE ETHICIST

My kindergarten-aged client has an IEP meeting scheduled for tomorrow. We received a draft of the Functional Behavior Assessment (FBA) and Behavior Intervention Plan (BIP) last night. I read in the BIP that the school is using a seclusion room called a "calm-down room," which the mother told me is a padded closet with a locked door.

Basically, a punishment procedure.

I find this to be extremely concerning and unethical.

Locked timeout rooms are banned in most states.

Was the BIP prepared by a BCBA? If so, that person has possibly violated 4.08 of the Code of Ethics.

4.08 Considerations Regarding Punishment Procedures

(a) *Behavior analysts recommend reinforcement rather than punishment whenever possible.*

(b) *If punishment procedures are necessary, behavior analysts always include reinforcement procedures for alternative behavior in the behavior-change program.*

(c) *Before implementing punishment-based procedures, behavior analysts ensure that appropriate steps have been taken to implement reinforcement-based procedures unless the severity or dangerousness of the behavior necessitates immediate use of aversive procedures.*

(d) *Behavior analysts ensure that aversive procedures are accompanied by an increased level of training, supervision, and oversight. Behavior analysts must evaluate the effectiveness of aversive procedures in a timely manner and modify the behavior-change program if it is ineffective. Behavior analysts always include a plan to discontinue the use of aversive procedures when no longer needed.*

Do we have any procedures in place for reporting or discouraging the use of this type of punishment procedure in public school settings?

School districts are an entity independent from the behavior analysis Code of Ethics, and they operate according to their own rules. However, behavior analysts who work for the school district must still adhere to the Code as do BCBAs who consult with the school district. In this case, this means making sure that the least restrictive procedures have been followed. At a recent conference, a presenter said that over 80% of BCBAs working in school districts have been pressured to violate our Code of Ethics, so you are not alone.

##

Four days later . . . from the behavior analyst.

Thank you so much for this information. The seclusion room procedure was added by the school psychologist. I requested, in advance of the meeting, that the district have their BCBA, Behavior Specialist, or equivalently positioned employee present at our meeting. The district does not employ any BCBAs, but did have their "behavior specialist" present at the meeting. I argued extensively for the removal of the seclusion room from my client's BIP, and the district did finally agree to remove it. Although I am very pleased with the outcome of the meeting for my client, I am horrified that this procedure is being used on other children within that school district.

##

A persistent theme in applied behavior analysis research over the past 20 years has been the search for alternatives to the use of punishment. The development and widespread adoption of functional analysis as a method for discovering motivational operations (MO) has demonstrated that if we understand the MOs, we can reduce or eliminate problematic or dangerous behaviors by eliminating the motivation for the behaviors to occur and then replacing them with behaviors maintained by positive reinforcement. This school district does not have a BCBA on staff and it appears that the timeout room was not initiated by a behavior analyst. The BCBA consultant acted quickly and argued persuasively that the use of this punishment procedure be removed from the student's BIP. It is quite discouraging that behavior analysts working in the schools are so often pushed to ignore our Code of Ethics at the expense of humane and effective procedures based on evidence-based research. If you work in a school setting, be wary when administrators tell you that your Code of Ethics does not apply in their schools: It does!

ETHICS QUESTION #10—RESPONSE FROM THE ETHICIST

I am a brand new BCBA who did not receive very good supervision when I was in training, but want to become a responsible supervisor. My company is headed by a BCBA who has supported me, but she does not actually work with clients and she is not up to date on the Code of Ethics.

This is a new requirement.

I was reading through 5.0 and was puzzled by 5.07 where it says, "Behavior analysts design systems for obtaining ongoing evaluation of their own supervision activities."

I don't know exactly what this means. I've asked the other BCBA who has been here a while and she didn't know either but she told me not to worry about it.

Can you tell me what this means and what I need to do to be compliant? I don't want to be in trouble with the BACB on my first job.

There are two key concepts here, "systems" and "evaluation" of your supervision activities. Systems refers to the idea that in an organization there are many moving parts that have to precisely coincide in order for there to be a reliable outcome. Effectively supervising one person involves:
1) Regularly scheduling observations of the individual as they carry out their behavior analysis duties.
2) Taking data on their performance using checklists.
3) Determining which aspects require improvement or modification.
4) Rank ordering those items.
5) Meeting with the supervisee and providing Behavioral Skills Training (BST).
6) Scheduling the next observation time.
7) Determining if the person showed improvement in the skill that was trained and starting the cycle over again. This system of supervision can be very powerful if used as described and has built into it the *evaluation* of your supervision routine.

As you come to step 7, you will know whether what you did during step 5 was effective, i.e. did the supervisee show improvement in the targeted skills? If so, your supervision method was effective and you can continue adding new skills. But, what if the supervisee did not improve? If this is what your data showed, then you need to revise your BST method, perhaps breaking the task into smaller steps or doing more role-playing or adding video feedback. You should evaluate your supervision tactics the same way you determine if the therapist is being effective with a client, you look at the client's data to see if there is improvement: If your supervisee is showing steady improvement over time, then your supervision is effective.

Now, back to the systems part of 5.07. The above description covers only one supervisee. Imagine if you have five or ten RBTs to supervise what will be involved in keeping all of this straight—this is where a system comes in. First, you will need a scheduling system to keep track of who is to be observed on each day and who is to receive BST. And, you will need a tracking system so you know what the priorities are for each person, and a graphing system so you can tell if your BST intervention is working *with each supervisee*. If your data shows that supervisees A, D and F are doing well but that B, C and E have not shown improvement over the last few weeks, you will need to change your tactics for B, C, and E. Your tracking system needs to prompt you to make changes that are individualized for each supervisee, and you need to keep close data on how those modifications work, for each person.

One way to think about a "system" is a self-regulating set of interlocking contingencies. A good method for beginning supervisors is to set up a system for *one* of your supervisees, make sure that all of the parts work, and then add a second and third supervisee. Setting up prompts for meeting with supervisees and having a data collection and graphing system to tell you how you are doing will keep you laser-focused on what you need to do to be an effective supervisor. Supervisors will need to be proficient with scheduling software as well as the use of checklists and spreadsheets with graphing capabilities. Behavior Skills Training is the recommended Best Practice for training supervisees to improve their skills. Traditional meetings with supervisees to discuss progress and shortcomings will not meet the requirements of 5.07.

ETHICS QUESTION #11—RESPONSE FROM THE ETHICIST

Hi!

I have a question regarding graduate programs and written academic policies and rules for authorship. In my country, an ABAI accredited graduate program in behavior analysis gives all of its master's students these written instructions for their master's theses: "In the event of publication, academic supervisors shall be acknowledged as co-authors." There is no mention of any contribution by the academic supervisors, as most notably mandated by APA and BACB ethical guidelines.

This is certainly counter to APA and the BACB Professional and Ethical Compliance Codes for Behavior Analysts.

9.08 Acknowledging Contributions
Behavior analysts acknowledge the contributions of others to research by including them as co-authors or footnoting their contributions. Principal authorship and other publication credits accurately reflect the relative scientific or professional contributions of the individuals involved, regardless of their relative status. Minor contributions to the research or to the writing for publications are appropriately acknowledged, such as, in a footnote or introductory statement.

I am thinking of addressing the department directly, and I am wondering if ABAI has any official policy beyond what is stated in the BACB ethical compliance code (such as the guidelines for The International Committee of Medical Journal Editors (ICMJE), The Vancouver-Group, etc.)?

ABAI does subscribe to the Code of Ethics of the American Psychological Association. The relevant part of that Code is printed below.

8.12 Publication Credit (APA Code of Conduct, 2017)
(a) *Psychologists take responsibility and credit, including authorship credit, only for work they have actually performed or to which they have substantially contributed. (See also Standard 8.12b, Publication Credit.)*

(b) *Principal authorship and other publication credits accurately reflect the relative scientific or professional contributions of the individuals involved, regardless of their relative status. Mere possession of an institutional position, such as department chair, does not justify authorship credit. Minor contributions to the research or to the writing for publications are acknowledged appropriately, such as in footnotes or in an introductory statement.*

It is important to note that since there is no official relationship between ABAI (which accredits behavior analysis programs) and the BACB which has established the Code of Ethics, this may be a loophole. You should go to the Contact Us page at ABAI and ask for an option: www.abainternational.org/contact-us.aspx

By the way, the majority of the supervisors are not Board Certified Behavior Analysts.

This provides an interesting twist. If they are not BCBAs, they do not come under the BACB Code of Ethics. Unless they are psychologists, the APA Code does not apply either. Do you have a similar professional organization in your country that might have a Code item that would cover this?

If your program states that they support the BACB Code of Ethics, you should approach your department and respectfully request that they revise their policy to be in line with the BACB Code of Ethics.

Both the BACB and the APA Codes of Ethics emphasize that authorship credit should be based on merit, i.e. the contribution each person on the research team makes to the final research product. If a supervisor has made a significant contribution, then of course this individual would be recognized. If supervisors or staff have assisted with the project but have not made a significant contribution, they might receive an acknowledgement in a footnote indicating they participated, but their names would not be included on the list of authors.

ETHICS QUESTION #12—RESPONSE FROM THE ETHICIST

I teach an Ethics course and we were just reviewing the compliance code. Could you give me any clarification on one of the Code items? In Code 10.02 (b), it talks about the need to report, "Any public health and safety related fines or tickets where the behavior analyst is named on the ticket." Could you give me examples of the types of tickets or fines this is referring to?

Here is Code 10.02 in its entirety . . .

10.02 Timely Responding, Reporting, and Updating of Information Provided to the BACB RBT

Behavior analysts must comply with all BACB deadlines including, but not limited to, ensuring that the BACB is notified within thirty (30) days of the date of any of the following grounds for sanctioning status:

(a) *A violation of this Code, or disciplinary investigation, action or sanction, filing of charges, conviction or plea of guilty or nolo contendre by a governmental agency, health care organization, third-party payer or educational institution. Procedural note: Behavior analysts convicted of a felony directly related to behavior analysis practice and/or public health and safety shall be ineligible to apply for BACB registration, certification, or recertification for a period of three (3) years from the exhaustion of appeals, completion of parole or probation, or final release from confinement (if any), whichever is later; (See also, 1.04d Integrity)*

(b) *Any public health-and safety-related fines or tickets where the behavior analyst is named on the ticket;*

(c) *A physical or mental condition that would impair the behavior analysts' ability to competently practice; and*

(d) *A change of name, address or email contact.*

Below is the basic information on self-reporting to the BACB:

What Must Be Reported (From BACB.com)

Within thirty (30) days, behavior analysts must report the following to the BACB:

1. *Any violation of the Compliance Code or disciplinary investigation, action, or sanction, filing of charges, conviction or plea of guilty or nolo contendre ("no contest") to charges by a governmental agency, health care organization, third-party payer, or educational institution.*

2. *Any public health-and safety-related fines or tickets where the behavior analyst is named on the ticket;*

3. *A physical or mental condition that would impair the behavior analyst's ability to competently practice; and*

4. *A change of name, address or email contact.*

Public health-and safety-related fines or tickets **must be reported** *to the BACB in the following circumstances:*

- *The incident or fine may indicate a physical or mental condition that could impact the competent delivery of services*
- *The incident or fine is evidence of another Compliance Code violation (e.g., a citation for negligently leaving a client unattended)*
- *The incident involved the operation of a motor vehicle and the fine was greater than $750*
- *A client was present during the incident (regardless of the amount of the fine)*
- *You were required to report the incident to your professional liability insurance provider*
- *You were required to report the incident to a client's third-party payer*
- *You were required to report the incident to a governmental regulatory board*

Public health-and safety-related fines or tickets **do not need to be reported** *to the BACB in the following circumstances:*

- *The incident does not name the behavior analyst as the "violator" (e.g., parking tickets, camera-based speeding tickets)*
- *The incident occurred at the location where behavior-analytic services are delivered but did not involve a client (e.g., a citation for violation of wage and hour restrictions, unemployment compensation claims)*
- *The incident involved the operation of a motor vehicle and named the behavior analyst, but did not involve any of the following:*
  - *a fine over $750*
  - *a client present during the incident or put at risk because of the incident*
  - *evidence of another Compliance Code violation*

(BACB Newsletter, November 2016, April 2017)

Self-reporting any changes to your status from a new address to a recent arrest must be reported to the Board within 30 days. So as to protect the public from a behavior analyst who might present a health or safety concern to clients, the Board requires specific self-reporting of the behavior analyst's being charged with or investigated for committing a crime or charges by a government agency. These incidents may be reported by others if it is known that the person did not self-report.

ETHICS QUESTION #13—RESPONSE FROM THE ETHICIST

I am the regional manager of an ABA program. I received the following ethics question from one of our BCBAs regarding an RBT on her team.

> The RBT's last day is Friday. Today she was given a going away gift from one of her client's preschool teachers.
>
> We know better than to take gifts from clients and their families, but we have never been offered a gift from another professional. The RBT refused the gift, but then the gift was placed in her bag when she wasn't looking.
>
> My question is, should we refuse all gifts from families and other professionals, or does this only apply to clients/families?

(margin note) The key word is "last day."

(margin note) Refuse gifts from *current* clients.

Code 1.06 (d) is referring primarily to BCBAs not accepting gifts from current clients where the gift might have some influence on their future professional judgment regarding treatment or supervision. Gifts from past clients or others who are not clients are not included in the gifting ban. Since the RBT is leaving the company, there could be no influence on her professional judgment.

1.06 Multiple Relationships and Conflicts of Interest [RBT]

(d) *Behavior analysts do not accept any gifts from or give any gifts to clients because this constitutes a multiple relationship.*

Behavior analysts work closely with clients often in their homes and are sometimes described as part of the family; the same happens with behavior analysts who work in or consult with schools where they are seen as part of the team and are invited to participate in social events and annual holiday parties. However, such close working conditions can lead to multiple relationships which are strongly discouraged by the Code of Ethics.

The rationale for Code 1.06 (d) is introduced in 1.06 (a, b, c), that is, giving and accepting gifts is characteristic of friendships rather than client and professional relationships. In order to prevent this form of dual relationship, behavior analysts are encouraged to discuss this with clients at the onset of therapy to avoid embarrassing situations later. Note that "gift" includes food and drink (yes, bottles of water) as well as tangibles such as gift cards and flat-screen TVs. (And yes, the flat-screen TV incident actually happened.) Behavior analysts are advised to consult the May 2015 BACB NEWSLETTER, pp. 1–2, for a further discussion of gifting and consideration given to the, "*intention* and effect of the gift."

ETHICS QUESTION #14—RESPONSE FROM THE ETHICIST

I am a BCBA in a school district. I consult with classrooms that serve students with emotional or behavioral disorders. I've been asked by an administrator who is not my supervisor to provide the academic curricula . . . for classroom teachers. I have a teaching credential and I feel that curriculum that includes functional skills, social-emotional skills, and behavioral skills falls within my scope of knowledge. However, I am having a hard time considering academic curriculum topics including math, social studies, English, and language arts to be within the scope of a BCBA. I am not working as a teacher, only as a BCBA. I have been offering assistance in structuring lessons to help support pro-social behavior and helping to monitor behavior during lessons. I was hoping for some assistance in determining whether or not curriculum development is within the scope of a BCBA. I have looked at the Task List for BCBAs and don't see . . .

Quite unusual.

It is a good idea to have a printed copy of the Task List handy.

anything remotely close to providing academic curricula for classroom teachers.

Here's the link to that list at the *BACB.com* site.

www.bacb.com/wp-content/uploads/2017/09/170113-BCBA-BCaBA-task-list-5th-ed-.pdf

You are correct. Developing classroom curriculum materials is not on the task list and is not one of the specialty skills that are the hallmark of our profession. In many school districts there might be as few as one BCBA per 400 students and the demands for functional assessments and effective behavior plans are such that they can barely keep up.

You could safely say, "I am sorry. This would require me to violate my Code of Ethics—1.02 Boundaries of Competence."

This administrator in this scenario would not be expected to understand our Task List or our Professional and Ethical Compliance Code for Behavior Analysts. There is a good chance that administrators have not even heard of the Code. In this case, the administrator may have known of the BCBA's previous experience as a teacher. Because the administrator needed some materials developed quickly, she might have acted without asking the BCBA if she would have a problem developing curriculum. This is not an unusual situation in schools where staff and administrators are short-handed and lack resources. Nonetheless, Code 1.02, Boundaries of Competence, provides a shield against requests that lie outside the scope of practice of behavior analysts. Even though the BCBA had been a teacher and had received some training related to curricula, 1.02 also means that BCBAs working as BCBAs should stay within the realm of providing services that are behavior analytic.

ETHICS QUESTION #15—RESPONSE FROM THE ETHICIST

Is there a clear-cut time when the BACB should get involved when an ethics violation has been made? For example, if I see a colleague (fellow BCBA) accept coffee at a client's house (a violation of Code 1.06 (d)), is this something I should report to the BCBA? I'm guessing the answer to this is no.

> Talk to the BCBA first.

You are correct. This is a violation, but you should first approach the person and address your concerns informally (according to Code 7.02 (c)). It is only when you have done this, (perhaps more than once), and you can see that this practice is impacting quality client services, that you should file a Notice. Note that you will need documentation for violation and it might be difficult to find a paper trail for such behaviors.

7.02 Ethical Violations by Others and Risk of Harm [RBT]

7.02 (c) If an informal resolution appears appropriate, and would not violate any confidentiality rights, behavior analysts attempt to resolve the issue by bringing it to the attention of that individual and documenting their efforts to address the matter. If the matter is not resolved, behavior analysts report the matter to the appropriate authority (e.g., employer, supervisor, regulatory authority).

> This is a real problem.

What if behavioral treatment is begun without consent? There is a real possibility of harm here, so I'm guessing maybe?

This is a clear violation which is mentioned several times in the Code of Ethics: 3.03, 4.02, 4.04. This happens a lot with behavior analysts working for school districts who believe they do not need consent to try any treatment.

Where is the line?

If there is any hint of harm to a client or a violation of their rights, it is time to first deal with it informally and then if it is not resolved, to file a Notice with the Board.

When we say any hint of harm to a client, we are generally talking about programs being done incorrectly, restraint being applied without parental approval, using extinction for a dangerous behavior, etc. We are not talking about physical abuse. In the case of the harm to the client being physical abuse or mistreatment, the proper legal authorities, abuse registry and Board should be notified immediately.

ETHICS QUESTION #16—RESPONSE FROM THE ETHICIST

Greetings! I find myself in a difficult situation and am wondering whether it falls into the realm of an ethical violation (albeit potentially minor) or simply poor professional etiquette.

I am in the process of identifying an appropriate home ABA provider for a family in our district. The family currently consults with a psychologist who is also a BCBA. The BCBA provides consultation regarding a medical desensitization program for their child and to assist the family in improving their communication with the school district.

While I was working with two providers to determine which would be the best fit with the student, the psychologist/BCBA, without any request from the school district to do so, sent an email to the entire educational team informing us that he/she had spoken to a former colleague who was a different home ABA provider about the case. The psychologist/BCBA said that this provider was available to take on the student's services.

So inappropriate and unethical.

The family is now demanding that this colleague-provider be contacted. I am very concerned the family will not accept any provider that isn't the one recommended by their outside BCBA.

Awkward!

In the meantime, the home services that were available to start next week are on hold while I contact this unsolicited provider.

In this case, did the psychologist/BCBA act unethically, violating 2.04 (a) . . .

Yes, the psychologist/BCBA committed a violation of 2.04 (a) of the Code of Ethics. He/she should *not* have made the phone call to his/her former colleague, thus possibly revealing confidential information about the family, and implying that he had something to do with the selection process. By doing so, he/she became a third party and thus comes under this section of the Code.

2.04 (a) When behavior analysts agree to provide services to a person or entity at the request of a third party, behavior analysts clarify, to the extent feasible and at the outset of the service, the nature of the relationship with each party and any potential conflicts. This clarification includes the role of the behavior analyst (such as therapist, organizational consultant, or expert witness), the probable uses of the services provided or the information obtained, and the fact that there may be limits to confidentiality.

acting outside of their role on the educational team, and potentially violating 1.06, engaging in a possible multiple relationship with this home provider while still working with the family?

This is correct.

Or was the psychologist/BCBA simply unprofessional in suggesting a different provider unsolicited thus adding conflict to an already charged dynamic?

This was definitely unprofessional. Also, it is unethical to discuss the case with someone else without written permission from the family as per Code 2.08 (" . . . never disclose confidential information without consent of the client . . .").

The third party in this scenario was a BCBA who was also a psychologist who took it upon him/herself to find a person for this position with the family. The psychologist/BCBA created a multiple relationship, conflict of interest (Code 1.06) with the family. And he/she did not disclose "the nature of the relationship with the BCBA" i.e. that he/she had not been authorized to make the phone call and was not in a position to recommend the former colleague for the position.

ETHICS QUESTION #17—RESPONSE FROM THE ETHICIST

Dear Ethics Hotline:

I ran across a BCBA on the internet who is advertising himself as certified in "Astronaut Training." At first blush, that seemed cool. But, upon investigation, I learned that this form of "Astronaut training" is simply another hyped-up version of sensory integration . . . therapy. With Astronaut Training, a client sits on a small platform that spins slow or fast, while the therapist plays ersatz "space-sounding music." It is totally bogus in my opinion—look it up yourself.

Several things bother me: (1) It appears that there is no peer-reviewed research to support Astronaut Training; . . . (2) Astronaut Training is derived from *sensory integration therapy*, which has little to no empirical support; (3) the conceptualization of behavior from a sensory integration perspective is diametrically opposite of our (behavior analysis) conceptualization of behavior; (4) by practicing this method, this BCBA is NOT putting behavior analysis *above all other professions* which I think is some kind of violation of our Code of Ethics.

> A BCBA supports this?

> You are correct.

Yes, it is certainly a violation; there are two Code items that are relevant here, 4.01 and 6.01.

4.01 Conceptual Consistency
Behavior analysts design behavior-change programs that are conceptually consistent with behavior analytic principles.

6.01 Affirming Principles[RBT]
(a) *Above all other professional training, behavior analysts uphold and advance the values, ethics, and principles of the profession of behavior analysis.*

This BCBA doesn't seem to be adhering to what he has learned in his research methods class in grad school about evidence-based practice. Plus, his clients to whom he delivers this Astronaut Training are not receiving "effective treatment."

Again, you are correct as described in 2.09 (a) of the Code of Ethics. Our clients served by Board Certified Behavior Analysts do have a "right to effective treatment."

2.09 Treatment/Intervention Efficacy
(a) *Clients have a right to effective treatment (i.e., based on the research literature and adapted to the individual client). Behavior analysts always have the obligation to advocate for and educate the client about scientifically supported, most-effective treatment procedures. Effective treatment procedures have been validated as having both long-term and short-term benefits to clients and society.*

"Effective" in behavior analysis means that there is substantial evidence in peer-reviewed journals using our methodology, i.e. single-case design research demonstrating experimental control using behaviorally based treatments.

What should I do?

The Code of Ethics specifies that you contact the BCBA directly and attempt an informal resolution, i.e. see if you cannot bring this person back into the fold of ABA. Perhaps he temporarily lost his way and forgot to use his analytical tools in sizing up this admittedly novel and cutely named form of therapy. Or, maybe the description on the website is not quite clear and the "Astronaut Training" was being used as a reinforcer in some way to teach new skills. In any event it is important that you make this contact and ask these questions first before reporting the person to the BACB. If you decide to do that you

would use the Notice of Alleged Violation form and outline the various Code items that have been violated as described above.

The BACB Code of Ethics is designed to help behavior analysts "stay within their lane" of treatment. The world is brimming with fads, frauds, and pseudoscientific as well as controversial and dangerous treatments for clients with ASD (Foxx & Mulick, 2016). The job of the behavior analyst is to be able to analyze these alternative "treatments" to see if there is any solid, peer-reviewed evidence that meets our high standards, i.e. can a treatment effect be demonstrated experimentally at the individual client level (Bailey & Burch, 2018). We have an obligation to educate our clients about these expensive, time-wasting methods and to evaluate them if the client insists on trying them.

2.09 (d) Behavior analysts review and appraise the effects of any treatments about which they are aware that might impact the goals of the behavior-change program, and their possible impact on the behavior change program, to the extent possible.

In this case, the behavior analyst discovered this anomaly (of a behavior analyst supporting sensory integration) and only had remote access to their approach via the internet as opposed to in person. Hopefully, she will be able to convince the BCBA that Astronaut Training is not a good fit for behavior analysis.

ETHICS QUESTION #18—RESPONSE FROM THE ETHICIST

I am looking at the possibility of beginning to offer remote supervision within my country (Australia) and I would like to know how the supervisory relationship relates to the supervisee's clients.

In Australia, there is a likelihood that some potential supervisees will be working independently or for companies that do not have behavior analysts on staff, which means there will likely be a high variability in service delivery. I am concerned that since supervisors are required to observe their supervisees working directly with clients during each supervisory period, the supervisor's responsibility will be extended to the quality and safety of the supervisee's clients as well.

> **Yes, the supervisor's responsibility will be extended to the quality and safety of the supervisee's clients. Behavior analysts should always be concerned about the quality of services and safety of the clients. In 5.0 of the Code of Ethics, you will find this clear statement, "When behavior analysts are functioning as supervisors, they must take full responsibility for all facets of this undertaking." This would include the quality and safety of the clients. Determining whether there is any risk to the clients being served by your potential supervisee should be a major factor in determining whether you would decide to accept them as supervisees in the first place. And, if there should be some turn of events where the environment became unsafe, you would need to become involved to remediate the situation. It is a big responsibility to take on a supervisee and this is why we do not recommend accepting this assignment lightly.**

What level of responsibility do supervisors have to the clients of an independent supervisee?

> **The supervisee you choose to work with is not "independent" as far as you are concerned. This person is *your* supervisee working with clients in a setting. When you are interviewing the supervisee, you would be advised to go to the setting to observe the operation. Size up the setting for safety, cleanliness, and suitability as a training site for the client and a workable setting in which you will provide supervision. You should be prepared to use the 5.01–5.07 items as your checklist to determine if you are qualified (5.01) for this supervisee and client. Also review other items in this section to make sure the setting/supervisee/client is a good match ethically.**

Supervisors play a huge role in the service delivery system. They are at the top of a pyramid of services that cascades down to BCaBAs and RBTs and then, of course, to the clients. So many things can go wrong which might adversely affect the person receiving treatment. For example, BCaBAs may not do their part in providing support to the RBT. The RBT may not be up to the challenge of providing consistent therapy day-after-day and accidentally reinforce an inappropriate or dangerous behavior or simply succumb to "behavior drift" so that the client gradually escalates a minor problem into a major problem. Staying directly involved with your team is a full-time job that warrants care and consideration in the selection of individuals who wish to become supervisees. One final tip would be if you are considering someone as a supervisee in a setting that is not yours, you would be well advised to speak to the administrator of that setting so they are fully aware of the situation. Administrators can support you in your role as a supervisor so if something comes up that interferes with the humane and ethical delivery of services, they will be supportive and take corrective action.

ETHICS QUESTION #19—RESPONSE FROM THE ETHICIST

Knowing that they are not evidence-based, should BCBAs be implementing treatments such as Zones of Regulation, and Social Behavior Mapping as treatments for children with autism?

> To provide some background information, the Zones "is a systematic, *cognitive behavior approach* used to teach self-regulation by categorizing all the different ways we feel and states of alertness we experience into four concrete zones. The Zones curriculum provides strategies to teach students to become more aware of, and independent in *controlling their emotions and impulses, managing their sensory needs, and improving their ability to problem solve conflicts.*
>
> By addressing *underlying deficits in emotional and sensory regulation, executive functions, and social cognition*, the curriculum is designed to help move students toward independent regulation. The Zones of Regulation incorporates Social Thinking® (www. socialthinking.com) concepts and numerous visuals to teach students to identify their feelings/level of alertness, understand how their behavior impacts those around them, and learn what tools they can use to manage their feelings and states."[2]
>
> As you can tell, this is not a behavioral approach to treatment and the limited group research that has been done does not meet *JABA* standards; if a BCBA was implementing "Zones" this would be a violation of Code 6.0 and 6.01 (a).
>
> *6.0 Behavior Analysts' Ethical Responsibility to the Profession of Behavior Analysis*
> *Behavior analysts have an obligation to the science of behavior and profession of behavior analysis.*
>
> *6.01 Affirming Principles* [RBT]
> a) *Above all other professional training, behavior analysts uphold and advance the values, ethics, and principles of the profession of behavior analysis.*
>
> Further, a search of the *JABA* index through the Wiley search engine shows that there are NO published behavioral studies on this approach.

Is this issue one that should be brought to the Board for review?

> The responsible, ethical thing to do is approach the BCBA and ask about this treatment strategy (take a copy of the Code of Ethics with you). Respectfully listen to the BCBA's answers. Then, bring up element 6.0 and 6.01 and 4.01 (Conceptual Consistency) of the Code to try to educate the BCBA on the need for *all* behavior analysts to follow the Code of Ethics. If the BCBA listens and agrees to correct the error, you might not have to report him/her to the BACB. If the BCBA says you are wrong and he or she plans to continue this unethical activity, you should then consider reporting the BCBA to the Board. To do this, you will need the Notice Form from the BACB.com website. Review the requirements for reporting someone and make sure you have all your documentation ready. This is a time-consuming task, but it is the only way to ensure that we have a strong, ethical profession.

##

One day later . . .
   Thank you for such a thorough response; it is extremely helpful. In Canada, specifically in Ontario, these two approaches are very commonly used and called ABA. Although I cannot make a provincial change, I hope to start small within my agency.

Fad treatments such as these pop up all over the internet with flashy websites and compelling testimonials. They usually have a complex theory of some sort to back them up as well. The combination of theory, website, and testimonials is enough to convince some parents to try these methods. Well-trained behavior analysts should be prepared to ask tough questions about the research on these approaches and reject them when there is no research. Several elements in our Code specifically address non-behavioral treatments. The general thrust of the Code of Ethics is that behavior analysts use only behavior analysis procedures and treatments. Our field has decades of experimental analysis of behavior science, and now we have over 50 years of well controlled ABA research published in *JABA* to help us determine what works and what doesn't. And, to be clear, neither of these approaches has anything to do with ABA.

ETHICS QUESTION #20—RESPONSE FROM THE ETHICIST

I am a parent and I have a question regarding ethics when it comes to charging fees. My wife and I recently reached out to a behavior analyst for our son who has been diagnosed with mild autism. The therapist sent us her fee schedule and we scheduled a phone-intake interview. We knew we were being charged for this interview, but I should make it clear that we have never signed anything saying that we understand how her fees work. She then proceeded, with our permission, to observe our son at school. We knew we would be charged for this as well. She also consulted with numerous other people on our son's team (teachers, speech therapist, etc.). Her fee schedule mentioned that she charges for any consultation time above 15 minutes.

This is a little unusual.

Before contacting these people, she never reminded us of this nor did she ask how long we would give her permission to be on the phone at our expense. We were not present for these phone calls so we had no control and she did not make the people being consulted aware of the charges.

This looks like a blank check.

She has now charged us a large sum for these calls as well as her calls to us beyond the initial phone interview. Basically, she has charged us for consultations that went beyond what we would have given her permission for had we been informed properly of this charge AND she is charging us for getting information on our child. This is a form of ransom, isn't it?

This is not technically ransom because ransom usually involves the person *taking* something from you first and then *offering it back* for a fee. But, if the point you are making is that you feel like you were taken advantage of, that is certainly understandable.

I am also a teacher and I know that my principal wouldn't dream of charging parents for teacher contact. It's expected, it's part of the job. We have spoken to numerous other BCBAs who have informed us that the above practices of this behavior therapist are not the standard.

Yes, this is correct. This type of phone consultation is usually not billed.

So, I guess my question is: Has this behavior analyst broken anything in your Code of Ethics?

Please take a look at 2.12 (a, b, c) and 2.13 of our Code of Ethics which is pasted here. The BCBA should have presented you with a printed, proposed contract for services in advance in which *all* the fees were spelled out to your satisfaction. It appears from your description that there were "hidden" fees that were not explained. Behavior analysts should be absolutely clear about their fees. We are professionals and don't want to be accused of being like a bank or phone company with hidden fees.

2.12 Contracts, Fees, and Financial Arrangements
(a) *Prior to the implementation of services, behavior analysts ensure that there is in place a signed contract outlining the responsibilities of all parties, the scope of behavior-analytic services to be provided, and behavior analysts' obligations under this Code.*
(b) *As early as is feasible in a professional or scientific relationship, behavior analysts reach an agreement with their clients specifying compensation and billing arrangements.*
(c) *Behavior analysts' fee practices are consistent with law and behavior analysts do not misrepresent their fees. If limitations to services can be anticipated because of limitations in funding, this is discussed with the client as early as is feasible.*

2.13 Accuracy in Billing Reports
Behavior analysts accurately state the nature of the services provided, the fees or charges, the identity of the provider, relevant outcomes, and other required descriptive data.

If she has, what can we do?

You can file a Notice of Alleged Violation with the BACB; to do so, go to *BACB.com* and search for the Notice form and file as instructed.

We will not be continuing with this therapist as her hidden expectations have put a bad taste in our mouths.

Have you tried putting your concerns in writing about the fees and asking for an adjustment?

Ethical behavior analysts endeavor to be transparent in every way with their clients from intake to assessment and treatment. Billing is a necessary part of that cycle and there should be no surprises in what the client will be charged. This client now sees this BCBA (and possibly our field) as dishonest and devious and will likely take this impression with them going forward. This could make it difficult for these parents to work successfully with a future behavior analyst they may encounter. Behavior analysts should earnestly strive to work honestly and openly with all clients bearing in mind that the impression we leave with clients can last a very long time.

ETHICS QUESTION #21—RESPONSE FROM THE ETHICIST

I had a question surrounding consent. I cannot seem to find an appropriate answer that directly cites the Professional and Ethical Compliance Code in some way. I am assuming that I should just err on the side of caution, anyway, but I would like to hear your opinion on the topic.

I have been a BCBA for one year now. I currently work for a company that contracts with schools for consultation, supervision, and assessment needs for multiple disciplines (BCBAs, School Psychologists, LICSWs, ABA therapy, testing services, etc.). I have a school that I am contracted with for 12 hours per week. Within this BCBA consultation, I complete any FBAs that the school needs conducted, and my remaining hours will be dedicated to helping observe and making suggestions for any students that they may be struggling with. For the FBAs, my company typically completes a separate Letter of Agreement and/or the schools receive a signed informed consent surrounding the assessment before I begin. My question is, for the other students that they are requesting . . . me to "help out" with, is it necessary that I also receive parental consent for observation and any plans suggested thereafter?

In schools an assessment is a test.

> **Yes, a significant part of "assessment" for behavior analysts is direct observation in the natural setting so as per Code 3.03 you would need consent from the parents of these children.**

3.03 Behavior-Analytic Assessment Consent

(a) *Prior to conducting an assessment, behavior analysts must explain to the client the procedure(s) to be used, who will participate, and how the resulting information will be used.*

(b) *Behavior analysts must obtain the client's written approval of the assessment procedures before implementing them.*

Your "client" is the student.

Or, do I operate under the premise that I am acting as a school employee and already have some kind of inherent consent?

> **No, it is not a safe position to assume you have *inherent* consent. You are a behavior analyst first and an employee second; your concern is for the rights of the student (in this case privacy) and the Code of Ethics which says that we ask for permission/consent to work with students. And, furthermore, as described in 3.03 (a) you, *"must explain to the client the procedure(s) to be used, who will participate, and how the resulting information will be used"* so simply having them sign a blanket consent form is not nearly enough permission.**

(I am unsure if a district-employed BCBA would need consent for these things, as well as compared to my position as more of a "third party" contract.) At which point in the . . .

> **Behavior analysts need consent regardless of where they work.**

consultation process does the school BCBA need consent to observe a particular student?

> **Yes, school BCBAs definitely need consent to observe a student since they would come under the Code regardless of who employs them. Consent is needed when an assessment or observation is asked for.**

No, before.

Would it be after observing . . . if further functional assessment and formal behavior plans are warranted? Or does the BCBA need a consent simply to observe?

Does this situation differ from a permanently hired district employee compared to my role as an outside contract employee?

Yes, consent is needed to observe a student.

> **Regular district employees do not have a Code of Ethics so they carry out their duties as instructed, but behavior analysts are professionals and we have a strong client-centered Ethics Code.**

My company is trying to research the correct direction to take this. With multiple disciplines hired within, it would be important that each employee . . . understands their obligation for obtaining consent, and if they need to delegate this responsibility to the schools before proceeding with any interaction with the student.

Ideally, all companies would be so responsible.

Each discipline has its own Code of Ethics and many are much less specific than the BACB Professional and Ethical Compliance Code.

Many school systems use a "blanket consent" form sent out to all parents at the beginning of the year to cover a wide variety of counseling or other therapeutic interventions and permissions for field trips, etc. This can be viewed as a "school-centric" tactic rather than a "client-centric" approach and primarily benefits the school since seeking individual permissions takes more work and more time. However, as described in this case, our Code of Ethics is very clear that our goal of being transparent in everything we do supersedes a rule designed for the convenience of administrators.

This question brings up many related issues and the interested reader may want to consult Codes 2.03, 2.05, 2.08, 2.15, 3.01, 4.02, and 9.03.

ETHICS QUESTION #22—RESPONSE FROM THE ETHICIST

I'm writing to you because I'm facing an ethical issue in my practice that I'm not sure how to handle. Over the past two months, through my place of work (an integrated preschool/ABA service provider), I have met with two families who would like to enroll their children in our program. Both of these families are currently receiving services from another ABA service provider, which is owned and operated by a BCBA.

Both of these families have volunteered information about the other service provider that I know conflicts with the Professional and Ethical Compliance Code. Neither set of parents were made aware of what these codes are or how they can lodge a complaint.

This in itself is a violation of the Code 2.05 (d).

2.05 Rights and Prerogatives of Clients ^{RBT}
(d) *Clients and supervisees must be informed of their rights and about procedures to lodge complaints about professional practices of behavior analysts with the employer, appropriate authorities, and the BACB.*

They are not aware that they have any options for recourse. My own BCBA supervisor (I'm not yet certified) has said that in those situations I can't directly explain to the parents how to lodge a complaint against their previous service provider. I can explain our policies here (which include informing parents of the code and explaining how to lodge a complaint), and leave it at that.

Actually, if the parents ask for help in filling out the form (you may have to download it for them from the BACB.com website) you *may* assist them; what you cannot do is *initiate* the complaint with them against another agency.

If the parents decide to use this information to lodge a complaint against their previous service provider, then that is beyond my area of concern.

No, your job is to watch out for the BEST INTEREST of your clients and if this means helping them file a Notice then that is appropriate under 7.02 (b).

(b) *If a client's legal rights are being violated, or if there is the potential for harm, behavior analysts must take the necessary action to protect the client, including, but not limited to, contacting relevant authorities, following organizational policies, and consulting with appropriate professionals, and documenting their efforts to address the matter.*

The thing I'm struggling with is this: At what point do the ethical violations I'm hearing about constitute enough of a problem that I, as a practitioner, have an ethical duty to intervene? These aren't small problems that I could solve with a gentle reminder to this BCBA. Complaints include shady billing practices, charging for services the parents haven't consented to, requiring parents to enroll in services outside the scope of ABA, not providing services that meet the standards for best practice, and one occasion where a child was hurt and they didn't follow proper protocol.

These are serious and warrant filing a Notice with the Board.

This is not even a complete list of the issues that have been brought to my attention by these parents. I am conflicted because I know that I can't directly instruct these parents to make a complaint.

Correct, but if they have not been informed of their rights by the previous BCBA then it becomes your obligation as described in 2.05 (d) above and to help them if they ask (which I'm sure they will).

However, I know that the likelihood of them initiating this process on their own is minimal, and this practitioner is still providing service to families and children in my city.

Any guidance would be greatly appreciated!

This is a touchy situation and one that we have not encountered previously. BCBAs have an obligation to explain Code 2.05 (d) in plain English and answer any questions that may result. That fundamental right was not explained to the clients and now a second behavior analyst may be required to assist the clients file a Notice under 7.02 (b) "*behavior analysts must take the necessary action to protect the client.*" The second behavior analyst should remember that she is to treat the information gleaned from the client as confidential in nature and not to be acted upon outside of the relationship with the client.

ETHICS QUESTION #23—RESPONSE FROM THE ETHICIST

I was recently excluded from authorship on a published paper on which I was supposed to be an author.

How did this happen?

The protocol is that all parties involved should be gathered together at the beginning of the research project to discuss authorship. Then they meet again at the end of the project to see if there are any adjustments. Some participants may be moved up since they made a greater contribution than originally expected, and others may move down the order since they played less of a role. In addition, all those who contributed sufficiently to be co-authors should have an opportunity to review drafts of the paper before it is submitted. They would remove it again when it comes back from the journal editor. Each participant then has multiple opportunities to be listed as a co-author. How did this not happen in your case?

I contacted the primary author and he said he would confirm I am an author if anyone ever questioned it. Is that the correct form of action when excluding an author from a published paper?

No, the primary author should contact the editor and request an error correction be published in the very next issue.

##

Follow up exchange days later . . .

Unfortunately, my issue was not resolved. It sounds like my co-author who originally excluded me mistakenly contacted the journal and the journal was the barrier to fixing the error as I found out myself as well. I eventually got into contact with the editor and then she spoke to the publisher who said they do not publish error corrections unless they address scientific inaccuracies. The first author and editor are both behavior analysts.

You must have been excited about being a co-author.

##

Behavior analysts who are involved in research should educate others ahead of time about the process of co-authorship to prevent this from happening. Are you still in touch with your "co-author"? Are you still doing research?

##

I do not have regular contact with the co-author anymore but I still do have his contact information. I am not doing research at the moment; I am focusing on other papers that need to be written up and submitted for publication but none of them are with the same author.

##

Some of the biggest rewards in our field come when we are in a "pro student" mode and looking for ways to help students get interested and involved in research. Eventually, we can help them move up the ladder of success to becoming an author or co-author on a study. This could help bright, ambitious undergrads get into graduate school or it could help grad students get a grant or assistantship. For students, having their names on a publication is THE mark of success as a researcher. Professors should recognize the importance of this recognition and do their best to promote the next generation.

ETHICS QUESTION #24—RESPONSE FROM THE ETHICIST

About a week ago, I met a person at a local autism fundraiser and he asked for my business card. When he saw that I am a BCBA, he commented on my credentials and said he is taking his exam in November.

He gave me his card and I didn't look at it until recently. He has his name followed by, BCBA(C). I feel like he is misrepresenting himself as a BCBA when he hasn't taken his exam yet and I've never heard of BCBA(C).

There is no "C" issued by the BACB.

Do I need to report this to the BACB?

You should start by following the advice in 7.02 (c) of the Code of Ethics and try to handle this informally. This would involve calling or writing to let him know that he is in violation of the Code. You could probably tell from his reaction to your conversation with him (defiant, defensive or apologetic, remorseful) if he is going to comply. If he has a webpage, you could check there to see if he corrected the problem.

7.02 Ethical Violations by Others and Risk of Harm [RBT]

7.02 (c) If an informal resolution appears appropriate, and would not violate any confidentiality rights, behavior analysts attempt to resolve the issue by bringing it to the attention of that individual and documenting their efforts to address the matter. If the matter is not resolved, behavior analysts report the matter to the appropriate authority (e.g., employer, supervisor, regulatory authority).

##

Five days later . . .

Thank you so much for your quick reply! I will get in contact with him about it.

He did not indicate what the "(C)" means. If he does when I talk to him about this then I'll be sure to update you.

Thanks again!

##

Follow up six days later . . .

Hi again,

I just wanted to update you that I contacted him about the business card and got a great reply. He was very apologetic and it was just a misunderstanding, so that's great! Thanks again for your guidance. Please see his reply to me below:

This is good news.

I apologize for not getting back to you yesterday; I appreciate you taking the time to contact me, I am aware of the issue and I apologize for the error. I have contacted my supervisor and our agency's graphic designer in order to correct the issue. There was an error in communication between our HR department and the graphic designer who handles all of our agency's business cards and website. My business card is supposed to say M. ABA (C), with the "(C)" standing for "currently enrolled."

I just received the business cards the Tuesday before the event where I ran into you, and had not noticed the error until this past weekend. I promise my intention was never to misrepresent myself as a BCBA. I am in the process of correcting the issue and was actually planning on contacting you this week. I have been compiling a list of everyone I believed to have given my business card to in order to inform them of the error. Additionally, I have brought the batch of business cards with the error back to the office to be disposed of, and am having new cards printed with the correction.

Moreover, I want to extend my sincerest apologies to you for placing you in the uncomfortable position of having to approach this issue. As I said above, it was never my intention to misrepresent myself and I take full responsibility for the error. I hope the situation did not damage any potential professional relationship.

Code 7.02 (c) was intended to have exactly this effect, one colleague who notices a potential ethical misstep on the part of another, approaches that individual in a friendly way and asks questions related to an observed incident. The first person should assume that perhaps they don't understand the situation and just want to clear some things up not to immediately put them on the defensive which could make matters worse. The second person in this case was honest enough to admit that an error was made and immediately took steps to correct the business card and additionally try to contact anyone that he happened to hand them out to; this is really taking full responsibility. There is certainly no need to file a Notice against the person in a case like this.

ETHICS QUESTION #25—RESPONSE FROM THE ETHICIST

There is a colleague who lives in the US and is Brazilian. She comes back to Brazil every now and then to teach "workshops" and constantly posts pictures from these workshops and the people who attend them on Facebook.

This is not allowed unless she gets permission from participants in writing.

In addition, on her Facebook page, she frequently posts pictures with supervisees and students.

When you say students, do you mean _clients_? If so, this is not allowed under the Code of Ethics is 2.06 (a).

If you are talking about college students, they should give written permission. For adults, she has to have a photo release signed by each person.

She also uses the BACB stamp when disseminating her workshop fliers. It appears that she is using the BACB's name to give her workshop an increased value or strength.

Are you talking about the ACE logo? Training providers must apply to become ACE Providers and are required to post the logo to verify that they have been approved and include a statement like this: "_____ is a Behavior Analyst Certification Board (BCBA) Authorized Continuing Education (ACE) provider # _____." If they do not include their authorized number, they are likely not approved. If they do include the number, they can be checked out with the BACB to see if they are currently approved. Further, if you have complaints about the training of an approved provider, be sure to include their number in your letter to the BACB.

10.03 Confidentiality and BACB Intellectual Property [RBT]
Behavior analysts do not infringe on the BACB's intellectual property rights, including, but not limited to the BACB's rights to the following:
(a) BACB logo, ACS logo, ACE logo, certificates, credentials and designations, including, but not limited to, trademarks, service marks, registration marks and certification marks owned and claimed by the BACB (this includes confusingly similar marks intended to convey BACB affiliation, certification or registration, or misrepresentation of an educational ABA certificate status as constituting national certification);

I have heard (but have no proof) that she has been publicizing that she is the only one in Brazil who can offer services based on Applied Behavior Analysis.

This is a violation of 1.04, Integrity, of the Code of Ethics. If you had proof, the person can be reported to the Board. When you say, "I have heard," this is considered hearsay and you can't do much about it. Without proof and only having the unsubstantiated reports of others, you are one step away from passing along a rumor.

Last year, one of her fliers stated she was a PhD. I wrote her to ask her to remove that information because she only has a master's degree.

This is good because you have met the requirements of 7.02 (c) (informal resolution). This is also a violation of 1.04, Integrity, of the Code of Ethics. If you have proof (e.g. a copy of the flier), the person can be reported to the Board.

People write me every week to let me know of something she has done, but I keep saying that if someone wants to report something they should write to the BACB.

It is good you told the people telling about the colleague to write to the Board themselves. Remember that only those with first-hand knowledge of the incident can file a Notice with the Board, and the person who is being reported must be a behavior analyst with Board certification.

My question is: Given everything that is on her Facebook page which is the only thing I have access to, should I report this person?

Certainly.

ETHICS QUESTION #26—RESPONSE FROM THE ETHICIST

Here is my question: Information for an upcoming school training has been disseminated. A well-known BCBA is the contact person. The training is on Social Thinking which does not have a solid research base but is frequently used in the autism treatment community.

> **Clients have a right to effective treatment as described in Code 2.09. A review of the *JABA* search engine (Wiley Online Library) going back 50 years does not find a single study on "Social Thinking." Further, in reviewing the "research" section of the Social Thinking website, it appears that there are no published, legitimate peer-reviewed studies there either.**

The BCBA is only responsible for taking questions and issuing CE credit for the professional development/ training. I'm unsure how much she was involved in the decision-making process prior to the training announcement (i.e. whether she recommended the curriculum, was involved in the conversations of whether or not it is evidence-based, how to advertise, etc.).

> **What is the BCBA's professional relationship with the people who are actually putting on the school training? Is she employed by the school system?**

I have been in contact with the BCBA to see if there was a way for her to distance herself from the training.

Code 7.02 (c).

Because we are in such a small state/community, even if she were not to use her BCBA credential, everyone knows she is a BCBA. She indicated that it would not be her place to provide a disclaimer that the curriculum is not evidence-based. I have since asked if there would be a way for her to no longer be the contact person.

> **The BCBA may not want to have conflict and ask for a disclaimer, however, she absolutely could do this.**

My concern is that promoting or appearing to promote this curriculum is not being consistent with the BACB Professional and Ethical Compliance Code specifically related to reliance on scientific knowledge (Code 1.01), being conceptually consistent (4.01), affirming principles (6.01) and disseminating behavior analysis (6.02).

What are some reasonable next steps? As I indicated, I am very much aware that the Social Thinking curriculum is very popular in the autism community and that many BCBAs are using it within a solid behavior context (operationally defining terms, taking data, etc.).

> **This treatment approach appears to be derived from the sensory integration movement that has brought us so many other fad treatments. You have made a good faith effort to resolve this informally (7.02 (c) of the Code) so you have good grounds for reporting this BCBA to the Board. Other relevant Code items are: 4.01, 6.01, 6.02, 8.01.**

Thank you for your time and any guidance you may have.

A few days later . . .

Thank you for your response to my question. I wanted to let you know what has happened since then. I drafted a letter to BACB and edited it several times before planning to send it. The BCBA contacted me the day I planned to email BACB. She reached out to the BACB herself and was given advice similar to the advice above. She opted to remove her name from the materials and did provide a disclaimer to the people with whom she works. However, I am unsure if she provided the disclaimer to those in attendance seeking continuing education for the event. Additionally, because we live and work in a very rural area, we have crossed paths from time to time and work on a few projects together. She has expressed her gratitude for discussing the concern with her. I am sure that not all stories end with such a positive ending.

Social Thinking is a very "hot" topic within schools right now. There are several others such as Zones of Regulation which are also not evidence-based.

Thank you for all your help.

Behavior analysts should always be aware that their reputation as evidence-based therapists can be tarnished by being paired with other approaches that are not as rigorous or are conceptually inconsistent with ABA. The first step in such cases is to approach the person informally, asking questions and raising concerns about this situation and attempting to persuade them to address the problem. The behavior analyst who submitted the question has responded appropriately in this situation, and received a very positive response. The behavior analyst will not need to file a Notice of Alleged Violation with the Code Compliance Committee of the BACB.

ETHICS QUESTION #27—RESPONSE FROM THE ETHICIST

Message to the Behavior Analyst Ethicist

Is asking employees to post a review on a recruitment website unethical? One of my employees expressed a concern so I wanted to check.

> **Yes, this would appear to be a violation of 1.07 Exploitative Relationships of the Code of Ethics. You are in a power position with respect to your employees and if they expressed themselves truthfully, e.g. "He's a nice guy but I think he might be bipolar. Some days he walks around all happy and smiling and the next, for no reason he will lock himself in his office and not respond to phone calls or email . . ." there is a good chance they would be demoted or fired.**

> *1.07 Exploitative Relationships* [RBT]
> *1.07 (a) Behavior analysts do not exploit persons over whom they have supervisory, evaluative, or other authority such as students, supervisees, employees, research participants, and clients.*

I don't know if this is a cut-and-dried question, or if you would like more context. The following is context from my perspective.

I emailed the entire company with the request and I have not mentioned it since. The website requires reviewers to indicate whether they are current employees.

> **Reviewers, to be considered objective, should be anonymous.**

So, there was no subterfuge. I did not tell them what to say or make any statements to insinuate either desirable or undesirable consequences based on their response. Is this ethical?

> **If you had suggested that reviews should be positive, this would really be a form of exploitation.**

There are subtle and not-so-subtle power relationships in all work settings. The chairman of the Board or a company owner can demand the CEO take in more and more clients even though staff are already stretched thin, the clinical director can overload BCBAs with time-consuming cases, and a BCBA can give RBTs "bad" assignments that involve a great deal of driving to in-home clients that are difficult to treat. Using people in these ways is a blatant form of exploitation and is a violation of the Code of Ethics.

And then there are subtle forms of exploitation such as this case shows. This request to employees to provide a review of the company in order to encourage behavior analysts to sign up is a subtle form of exploitation. The owner of the company seeing employee testimonials on other websites thought this was an acceptable practice, after all, he wasn't asking *clients* to post these reviews since he knew that was not allowed. But, since the owner was in a position to know who wrote the review, employees would be reluctant to tell the truth about working there for fear of losing their jobs or being harassed by management (which would likely terminate anyone who wrote a bad review).

ETHICS QUESTION #28—RESPONSE FROM THE ETHICIST

I have an ethical situation I would like some advice on to help ensure that I am acting appropriately.

Two months ago, I put in my 30-days-notice with my previous company.

In writing and you have a copy? Did you inform your BCBA supervisor too?

I worked for the company as a BCaBA assisting the BCBAs. During that notice time, no one from the company contacted me about transitioning a client to a new provider. The company did not even contact the client's parents to schedule transitioning to another 1:1 provider, until my final week.

Someone dropped the ball.

On my last day working for the company, an RBT contacted me to ask questions about what she was supposed to do with that client and mentioned him by name. She said she got my phone number from the client's parents. I informed her that I was no longer a contractor with the company and that any programming and treatment decisions needed to come from the current team on the client's case. I told her to ask one of the company owners or the BCBA on the case to discuss with her what needed to be done with the client.

Is there *any* chance that they never received your 30-day-notice? Did you sign a non-compete clause in your contract?

In March 2017, I received a very nasty email from one of the owners, claiming that . . .

This sounds like harassment.

> *1.05 (e) Behavior analysts do not knowingly engage in behavior that is harassing or demeaning to persons with whom they interact in their work based on factors such as those persons' age, gender, race, culture, ethnicity, national origin, religion, sexual orientation, disability, language, or socioeconomic status, in accordance with law.*

for three years I've never turned in any session notes and that they were keeping my final paycheck and were going to report me to the "proper agencies." I responded that she needed to check the email messages from early March in which I submitted documentation for 2015 through February 2017. I also said that the remainder of the documents had been uploaded into the company database from February until I left the company.

Do you have a copy of this correspondence?

In February 2017, the company conducted an internal audit and saw that I was missing documentation. I provided all of the missing documentation that was requested back in early March 2017. The owner has not responded to that email.

If it was via email I would send it again with "2nd Attempt" in the subject line.

I also saw on my final Year-to-Date statement from early March they withdrew a $100 administrative charge to "upload documentation and notes into the data base."

Later the same day I sent the email in March, I got a call from the executive director who told me that after he read the email that was sent he "knew where this was going" and wanted to intervene. I explained to him that I knew this was just a ploy to try to keep my final paycheck; this is a regular business practice with this company. (I have documentation from previous technicians who've left this company asking me why they weren't getting their final paychecks.)

Yes, this type of harassment is fairly common as a punisher. However, it is illegal in some states. You should check on this.

I have email correspondence between myself and a co-owner of the company in which I pointed out that immediately after I put in my final notice, an administrator reduced my pay rate by almost $10 an hour for one insurance company, and for a second insurance company they reduced it to $0.00. The co-owner emailed me back stating he would fix this. He did not say it was an accident or deny that an administrator went back and illegally adjusted the codes.

This is fairly common.

It is now June. Yesterday morning, I emailed the executive director to put our phone conversation in written format and to confirm with him that he told me that he "knows it is illegal to try to withhold someone's paycheck" and that he was going to work to settle this as quickly as possible. He has not responded to my email.

Yes, this is correct.

Last night, I got a call from another behavior analyst asking me to discuss the same client that the technician called me about. I explained to him that I no longer work for the company and that it would be a HIPAA violation to discuss this client.

He stated that the Board (BACB) requires me to work with him to transition this client to him.

You are correct, unless there was some other stipulation in your contract.

Keep a copy of your contract in a safe place.

I stated that the transition was to be done during my 30 days' notice period and he said the company was unable to find anyone until now. At this point, I told him I would contact the BACB for guidance on this situation and would follow any suggestions and recommendations they made.

Please note that the authors do not work for the BACB. If you want an official response from the BACB, you would need to write to the Board via their "Contact Us" link.

I'm sorry for this very long message but I feel like I'm being harassed and that they are . . . trying to get me to violate HIPAA as well as to work without pay. I would just like some advice.

Yes, you are.

You should immediately create a timeline (with specific times and dates) of what happened and attach your documentation on each step to show that you were operating in good faith. If you had a conversation over the phone, try to recall verbatim how it went, and commit it to paper so there are no significant gaps in your timeline.

Jon S. Bailey note: It is my opinion that from what you have described, you have not violated the BACB Code of Ethics. It appears that you have operated in good faith throughout this trying situation. In a case similar to yours, the company sued the BCaBA and she had to produce all of the documentation to show she had done her due diligence. That case was finally settled out of court and she was vindicated. If you have reason to believe that the company might sue you, you should consult an attorney in advance to see if there is anything else you need to do. Also, if any of the parties you mentioned are Board Certified Behavior Analysts, you may want to consider filing a "Notice" against them with the Board since it is clear that they violated the Code of Ethics in several respects. If they are not certified, then sadly, there is very little the Board can do.

It has become a standard in the field to give 30-days-notice to your company when you plan to resign. You must also offer to assist in the transition of your clients to another BCBA or to another provider. It is not appropriate for the company to wait until the last minute and then harass a behavior analyst who is operating in good faith. This is a violation of 1.05 (e) and is a reportable offense. It is quite unusual for a company to "go dark" during the 30-day period; they would normally have someone in the company immediately contact the BCBA and make plans for the transition. In this case, the company is clearly responsible for transitioning the client, not the BCBA.

Finally, with regard to our question above, "Is there any chance they never received your 30-day-notice?" any time behavior analysts (or other professionals as well) are resigning from a position or sending other important information, it is always best to do this through the regular mail by way of Certified Mail—Return Receipt Requested. An email can be sent as a backup, but the Certified Mail-RRR provides legal proof and leaves no doubt that your resignation was received.

ETHICS QUESTION #29—RESPONSE FROM THE ETHICIST

I work in a school district where a parent contacted the BCBA and said she won't consent to the initiation of services. May the BCBA initiate services at school without the parent's consent if directed to do so by the school district?

Even though a BCBA is employed by a school district, his or her primary commitment is to the client, in this case the student. When a BCBA is considering a position with a school district, we recommend taking a copy of the Code of Ethics to the interview. At the interview, BCBAs should point out the sections they are required to follow so as to head off any conflicts later. This meets the requirement that behavior analysts "make known their commitment to this Code" and take steps to "resolve the conflict in a responsible manner" under 1.04 (e) of the Code.

1.04 Integrity [RBT]
(e) *If behavior analysts' ethical responsibilities conflict with law or any policy of an organization with which they are affiliated, behavior analysts make known their commitment to this Code and take steps to resolve the conflict in a responsible manner in accordance with law.*

Note that BCBAs are committed first and foremost to the Professional and Ethical Compliance Codes for Behavior Analysts which clearly specifies that clients, in this case parents, must give consent for an assessment (Code 3.01, 3.03), and for the development of a behavior plan (Code 4.02).

4.02 Involving Clients in Planning and Consent
Behavior analysts involve the client in the planning of and consent for behavior-change programs.

Behavior analysts need to constantly keep in mind who their client is, in this case their client is the parent and obviously the student who would be the recipient of behavioral services. While the school may be the employer, it may not demand that the BCBA violate their Code of Ethics in the course of doing their job. School officials cannot be expected to know or understand our Code of Ethics so meeting with them to educate them on the limitations of what we can and cannot do is essential in this venue. Conflicts such as this one can come up between an ethical behavior analyst in any treatment setting whether it is a clinic, in-home, or a community setting. It is important to realize when behavior analysts compromise their ethics on one point of contention that there will surely be others. Before long, a BCBA who has not adhered to the Code on one point will be sliding down the slippery slope to unethical conduct.

ETHICS QUESTION #30—RESPONSE FROM THE ETHICIST

I am a BCBA and I co-own an ABA company in the Southeast. I was previously working for another company in the area as a case supervisor. We'll call the company "Company A." Although I never signed a formal contract with Company A, one of the co-owners of my current company signed a contract that pertains to BCBAs. This contract was very vague, but there was a non-compete clause in this contract.

Did your co-owner asked to be released from the non-compete?

We have not been soliciting previous clients in any way, but over the past few months I have had almost all of my clients independently contact us about leaving Company A and coming to our new company. We initially turned away these clients because we wanted to make sure legally and ethically we are not taking clients from our previous company too quickly. We have been referring these clients to another provider in the area because they are not happy with the services being provided at Company A. We have told them truthfully why we feel we can't take them as clients at this time. Some of the clients have chosen to wait until we are ready to take former clients at our new company. We told them we will keep them updated about when we are able to do this.

Asking former clients to leave their company and come to yours would be soliciting and should not be done. It does not appear that you are doing this. If former clients contact you and want to move your company, you should tell them to put this is writing and to specifically mention that they were not solicited in any way.

> Also referred to as *poaching*.

Our biggest question is what a safe time limit would be to take on these new clients. We have some parents that are very upset and are having a hard time understanding why they can't choose which provider their child and their family uses. It is like the families are indirectly under a non-compete! This has been a hard question for me to answer.

It is not a matter of time but of protocol as described above.

We have consulted a few different lawyers and they have looked at different cases under our state law. It seems that this subject is very up in the air.

Non-compete might be up in the air but not solicitation, that is fairly clear as per the guidance above.

I know health providers are generally not able to be held under non-competes in court, and I'm not sure if we would technically be considered health providers as BCBAs.

Yes, but you did not sign a non-compete. Your co-owner should seek to have this resolved with the previous company. As your attorney has told you, non-competes are not enforceable in all states and where they are it depends on the industry. Most often, the non-compete has to do with an employee taking proprietary information with them which really can't happen in ABA since all of our knowledge is public via journals, books, and conferences.

Have you run into this in another situation? We are also looking for guidance on what to tell families. It's hard to turn these families away when they're clearly not happy with their current provider.

See the comments above.

Another question we have is about Google and Facebook reviews. We are very familiar with our ethical code when it comes to testimonials and reviews. When trying to boost our site optimization in order to show up on search engines, we have read that a big component is having reviews on Google, Facebook, etc. We know that current clients can never give us reviews and that reviews have to specify if they're solicited or unsolicited. Is there an ethical way for us to still have reviews on Google/Facebook? We have been turning the reviews off, or reporting them to have them removed. I have noticed that other providers have reviews. Of course, complying with our ethical code would be our number one priority, even if that means we're a little lower on the Google search! We are wondering if we can still have reviews.

You cannot solicit reviews from current clients and should not do so from former clients unless you use the disclaimer in Code 8.05. However, you can put a disclaimer on your social media site that says, "We do not solicit testimonials from current or former clients. Any reviews posted here are purely at the choosing of those who we have worked with . . ." or something similar. The First Amendment still holds in commerce.

8.05 Testimonials and Advertising ^{RBT}

Behavior analysts do not solicit or use testimonials about behavior-analytic services from current clients for publication on their webpages or in any other electronic or print material. Testimonials from former clients must identify whether they were solicited or unsolicited, include an accurate statement of the relationship between the behavior analyst and the author of the testimonial, and comply with all applicable laws about claims made in the testimonial.

Behavior analysts may advertise by describing the kinds and types of evidence-based services they provide, the qualifications of their staff, and objective outcome data they have accrued or published, in accordance with applicable laws.

Thank you so much for your time and for your help.

##

Ten days later . . .
   Thanks again for all of your help throughout the past couple weeks. I ended up sending an email to all of my former clients' families explaining to them that I was no longer on their case. I am glad I did this, because from the emails I am receiving, the BCBA who is the owner of Company A still has not met with my past client's families and told them that I am no longer the BCBA on the case. I have had multiple parents email and call me asking for "advice" or "help." I was hoping you could give me some guidance on what I can and cannot communicate with these parents. I know I am not allowed to give them advice.

You can answer certain questions, but since you no longer have a professional relationship with these parents, giving no advice is your best policy.

I understand that I cannot solicit these clients to come with me to my next place of work as well.   _Correct._
   Do you have any recommendations on what I can say to these parents?

Yes, you can say that you left the company due to circumstances beyond your control and that you are now at another agency. If *they ask you* where you are, you can tell them. If they say, "We would like to keep working with you . . . " tell them that for ethical reasons they need to put that request in writing and send it to your new agency. You might also tell them that they may not be assigned to you as clients since that type of decision is made by the clinical director.

##

This question embodies three fundamentals of business practice in ABA. The first has to do with "non-compete" clauses (NCC) in employment contracts, also known as restrictive covenants. The purpose of this type of contract provision is to protect the employer from an employee who might leave the company and take confidential information with them to another company or start their own business. In behavior analysis, we have no "confidential information" (except client lists) since all of our treatments are based on evidence that is public in journal articles and books as well as methods and practices that are described in workshops and talks at conferences. The primary reason for employers using NCCs is to keep employees from leaving and going somewhere else to work but this may be seen as a restraint-of-trade practice. In addition, many behavior analysts may discover after a few months that their new company, much to their chagrin, is engaging in unethical professional and business practices; quitting under these circumstances may disallow the NCC because the company already breached the Code of Ethics. BCBAs finding themselves in this situation should contact a contract attorney and seek their advice on how to handle a departure without having to pay a stiff penalty or move hundreds of miles away to practice.

The second issue has to do with a BCBA leaving a company and taking clients with them. This is the great fear of an agency, the primary reason for the NCC, and is often referred to as "poaching" or stealing clients. If a company wants to prevent this from happening they would need to include a "non-solicitation" clause in their contracts. But, if an employee leaves a company and the clients contact *them* and ask to move with them it would not be considered "solicitation." Furthermore, a behavior analyst moving to a new company should not promise that if the families follow them that they will be their BCBA, that decision will be made by the owner or clinical director. Those clients would need to send a letter to their current company terminating the client relationship and asking that their files be transferred to ABC company without mentioning their former BCBA.

The third issue has to do with testimonials by current or former clients. Behavior analysts should recognize that testimonials are not evidence-based statements of fact, they are at best anecdotes and at worst made-up stories that have little real attachment to the truth. In their daily lives, behavior analysts are besieged with wild claims for products and services that are easily dismissed as a figment of the marketing department's imagination. Behavior analysts are critical thinkers who can see right through the smoke, such as those endorsements by actors posing as doctors, seniors with aching backs, and teens with acne reading cue cards written by advertising firms that don't impress us. Why then would we think that a testimonial drafted by a newbie in the HR department or a parent eager to impress management would have any validity? The best advice here is to follow the second paragraph in Code 8.05: Provide descriptions of your evidence-based services, detail the qualifications of your behavior analysts, and provide objective, verifiable outcome data.

ETHICS QUESTION #31—RESPONSE FROM THE ETHICIST

I hope this email finds you well. I am reaching out once again, as your guidance and suggestions in the past have worked tremendously.

I am a BCBA and business owner of an ABA clinic in South Florida. Unfortunately, I have received four resignations within the past month, and some of the staff have said that they're being offered $10+ an hour over what I am offering and some are Independent Contractor positions. With the first resignation, I began completing an exit interview asking what we could have done better and what made them decide to resign, so I am hoping to make some future changes to my business.

This is a problem if they are RBTs.

However, I am a bit concerned, since I have been participating in a Facebook group where this has been discussed and many people have expressed the high rates of burnout in the field recently. My question to you is: Can RBTs be classified as Independent Contractors or should they be all employees regardless of the number of hours worked per month?

This is a fairly common question.

RBTs cannot be Independent Contractors (IC). IC is an Internal Revenue Service (IRS) designation which says if you have to be supervised in your job, you cannot be an IC. It really has nothing to do with how many hours a person works, the issue is with supervision. See below for an IRS statement on this.

People such as doctors, dentists, veterinarians, lawyers, accountants, contractors, subcontractors, public stenographers, or auctioneers who are in an independent trade, business, or profession in which they offer their services to the general public are generally independent contractors. However, whether these people are independent contractors or employees depends on the facts in each case. The general rule is that an individual is an independent contractor if the payer has the right to control or direct only the result of the work and not what will be done and how it will be done. The earnings of a person who is working as an independent contractor are subject to Self-Employment Tax.

If you are an independent contractor, you are self-employed. To find out what your tax obligations are, visit the Self-Employed Tax Center.

You are not an independent contractor if you perform services that can be controlled by an employer (what will be done and how it will be done). This applies even if you are given freedom of action. What matters is that the employer has the legal right to control the details of how the services are performed.

If an employer-employee relationship exists (regardless of what the relationship is called), you are not an independent contractor and your earnings are generally not subject to Self-Employment Tax.

However, your earnings as an employee may be subject to FICA (Social Security tax and Medicare) and income tax withholding.

For more information on determining whether you are an independent contractor or an employee, refer to the section on Independent Contractors or Employees.[3]

I ask because I've heard mixed responses from those on the Facebook group, so I am unsure what we should be doing legally.

There is also a California Supreme Court decision on this that spells out clearly the requirements for ICs (see below).

4.1.18 California Supreme Court Ruling
So, what did the California Supreme court say this week?

Chief Justice Tani Cantil-Sakauye laid out three things a business must show for a worker to be classified an independent contractor:

1. *The worker is free from the control and direction of the employer*
2. *The worker performs work that is outside the hirer's core business*
3. *The worker customarily engages in "an independently established trade, occupation or business."[4]*

Your guidance will be much appreciated!

There are strong economic advantages for assigning RBT staff to Independent Contractor status rather than employees. The savings are estimated to be 20–30% versus the cost if they were regular employees. A disadvantage to the RBT is that they have to take care of their own taxes which they may not realize at the time is a substantial amount of money each month to set aside. Their paycheck looks larger as an IC but that is deceptive. Some companies have their head in the sand about this illegal practice and just want to deny it is a problem, "Everyone does it so how can it be illegal . . .?" is a common reaction when the ethical and legal issues are presented. The bottom line is that assigning RBTs to IC status is a violation of IRS rules and 1.04 (d) of the Code.

ETHICS QUESTION #32—RESPONSE FROM THE ETHICIST

Our agency has not been involved in formal IRB-approved research at this point in time, however, one of our BCBAs took a strong interest in a particular topic and sought out an expert in our field in that area. This expert ended up asking if our BCBA would be interested in helping generalize his results into natural settings (as we have many BCBAs placed in public schools where this research hasn't been conducted yet) saying our staff could be first author on the article.

> Is this "expert" a BCBA?

If research is proposed for schools, it usually also has to go before the school district research review committee.

He was able to add one of her cases onto an existing IRB approval and then set up one of his doctoral students to support her in implementing this. So far, this has only been through phone support. Our BCBA has attended several of the expert's training sessions over the last two years. The BCBA has done a lot of implementation related to the topic and has read the limited amount of research the expert has published. We thought the doctoral student was going to be present with the BCBA to run IOA. However, after having already started the project . . .

Was consent for this project received from the school district and principal and the parents as well?

the expert indicated that our staff could only move forward with the research/IRB work if we paid him to do an intensive and expensive training session he would conduct because he can't publish anything without first saying that the person running it is well trained.

Training should have been built in at the front of the project with a written agreement. That is not the way that this is done. The researcher applies for and receives a grant and then finds a setting. Then, the research is run at no cost to the setting. This could be considered a violation of Code 9.01.

9.01 Conforming With Laws and Regulations ^{RBT}

Behavior analysts plan and conduct research in a manner consistent with all applicable laws and regulations, as well as professional standards governing the conduct of research. Behavior analysts also comply with other applicable laws and regulations relating to mandated-reporting requirements.

We certainly agree that fidelity is crucial as is training, however, we are questioning if this is now creating a bias and crosses some ethical lines. Paying the expert to do this would create a different vested interest in the positive results. His IRB approvals are all run through a university, but it is a bit unclear if this training is just his own or run through the university as well.

It would be easy enough for you to call the chair of the IRB at the university and ask about this proposed project. You can also ask the question about payment. You will probably hear an audible gasp on the other end of the phone.

Am I overanalyzing this?

No, you seem to have just the right level of skepticism.

I was just a bit taken aback and felt we were teased along and once we were engaged in the project, the expert began looking for a sale rather than doing research.

This sounds very much like a commercial operation rather than a research endeavor and may be a violation of Code 9.02 (k).

9.02 (k) Behavior analysts avoid conflicts of interest when conducting research.

Additionally, if he is serious about this, wouldn't he want to send himself or someone he knows is competent in all of this out to run IOA rather than just having us do it all of it alone?

Certainly.

Is he requiring the training for that reason and it's normal for people to pay to be able to execute research?

Jon S. Bailey: I have been involved with behavior analysis research for nearly 50 years and I have never heard of an arrangement like this. This could be construed as a violation of Codes 9.02 (b) and 9.02 (d).

9.02 (b) Behavior analysts conducting applied research conjointly with provision of clinical or human services must comply with requirements for both intervention and research involvement by client participants. When research and clinical needs conflict, behavior analysts prioritize the welfare of the client.

9.02 (d) Behavior analysts plan their research so as to minimize the possibility that results will be misleading.

I'm concerned after paying all this, he can then turn around and upsell us again by saying our staff wasn't demonstrating competency and needs to do further training for more money.

You could let him know that you have run into a bureaucratic roadblock and then stop contacting or responding to him. In a few weeks, he will probably move on. Have you looked at a recent issue of *JABA*? The journal has a new section called, "Replications" where they are now willing to publish studies which are attempts to replicate previous studies. Consider if this would be an appropriate route for you. Is this "expert" a BCBA?

##

Follow up two months later . . .

We reached out to the expert/researcher, who was a BCBA-D, to get some clarification and to eliminate the middle man and potential for misinterpreted or misconstrued messages. The expert went dark and didn't respond to multiple requests to chat. We ended the project at the school somewhat simultaneously due to the student being placed out of district prior to us really being able to start anyway.

This is a very unusual situation. When conducting research in applied settings, the university-based faculty member will first approach the settings where she would like to carry out the study. She or he will talk with the administrators and other potential participants about the proposal and what their involvement will be so they are very clear of what they might be expected to do and how much time it will take. If they agree to participate, the name of the organization, in this case the school, will be included in the grant that the researcher prepares and then submits first to the university IRB and then, if approved, to the granting agency. The participants are not expected to in any way fund the research. At most they will provide "in kind" contributions of space, staff, and possibly use of some equipment.

ETHICS QUESTION #33—RESPONSE FROM THE ETHICIST

I have a question concerning the ethics of accepting or discharging clients from ABA services.

I am taking over the caseload of another BCBA and I have a new-to-me client. The client is an adolescent male who receives a low number of service hours (two per week). He has been working on an eye-contact program for a year with his first BCBA and has not made progress.

> Not a good sign.

Last week he made a gun threat at school and was suspended pending a psychological evaluation. The evaluation has already been done but we have not received any results.

Any threat regarding a gun is not to be ignored. Report this immediately to the proper authorities.

In the past, this client has made similar threats in the clinic before regarding our staff. I have not witnessed this but multiple techs have reported it.

> Reported to authorities?

The majority of the line techs are now afraid to work with him, and to be honest, I don't blame them. I don't want to over- or under-react to this.

In the middle would be good rather than over- or under-reacting. Put this in writing to local authorities.

Is it ethical to refer the client for psychological services given his lack of progress on his goals here?

Yes, this client should be referred for psychological services.

He has not officially been transferred to my caseload yet, and before this incident I had ideas for changes to his programming that might increase his success.

Unless you have expertise in this area, do not take this case. There is not anything in the ABA literature about how to treat something like this and *we* are the evidence-based people.

Now I'm wondering if ABA is right for him, and also whether recent events in the news are clouding my clinical judgment. Please advise!

The ethical thing to do here is to follow the guidance of Code 2.01 and 2.03 (a).

2.01 Accepting Clients
Behavior analysts accept as clients only those individuals or entities whose requested services are commensurate with the behavior analysts' education, training, experience, available resources, and organizational policies. In lieu of these conditions, behavior analysts must function under the supervision of or in consultation with a behavior analyst whose credentials permit performing such services.

2.03 Consultation
(a) Behavior analysts arrange for appropriate consultations and referrals based principally on the best interests of their clients, with appropriate consent, and subject to other relevant considerations, including applicable law and contractual obligations.

This question has to do with accepting a client or discharging him and making a referral to some other professional. In this case, the potential for gun violence is not to be ignored and is not the purview of behavior analysis. BCBAs should always be careful not to think that they can take on any and every case that comes their way since it could have serious consequences for the client and for the behavior analyst as well. ABA is not a cure-all for any and all "behavior" problems. Threats of gun violence should not be taken as verbal operants that can be put on extinction or simply replaced with more appropriate tacts, mands, and intraverbals. The incidence of school shootings is alarming and we need to play our part by alerting officials of any sign of this sort of precurrent verbal behavior.

ETHICS QUESTION #34—RESPONSE FROM THE ETHICIST

I witnessed a BCBA behave physically aggressive toward my student.

She crossed his arms over his body while he was on the ground and when he got up his lips were blue. I am not sure which ethical code this violates if any. I need guidance on proper documentation and how I can go about reporting her.

[Did anyone else see this?]

This sounds like a restraint procedure. Was it part of the client's behavior plan? Code violations could be cited in 4.08 or 4.09.

4.08 Considerations Regarding Punishment Procedures

(a) *Behavior analysts recommend reinforcement rather than punishment whenever possible.*

(b) *If punishment procedures are necessary, behavior analysts always include reinforcement procedures for alternative behavior in the behavior-change program.*

(c) *Before implementing punishment-based procedures, behavior analysts ensure that appropriate steps have been taken to implement reinforcement-based procedures unless the severity or dangerousness of the behavior necessitates immediate use of aversive procedures.*

(d) *Behavior analysts ensure that aversive procedures are accompanied by an increased level of training, supervision, and oversight. Behavior analysts must evaluate the effectiveness of aversive procedures in a timely manner and modify the behavior-change program if it is ineffective. Behavior analysts always include a plan to discontinue the use of aversive procedures when no longer needed.*

4.09 Least Restrictive Procedures

Behavior analysts review and appraise the restrictiveness of procedures and always recommend the least restrictive procedures likely to be effective.

You will need a witness who will sign a notarized statement that they saw this happen plus any written documentation, e.g. an incident report submitted at the time of the event.

[A witness is critical.]

Since your goal is to prevent future occurrences, you may want to consider first handling this informally according to 7.02 (c) of the Code.

If you do decide to file a complaint against the person, be sure and check the Notice form on the BACB.com website so you know what is involved, e.g. this is not anonymous and it could take a while for the BACB to process your complaint.

##

Five minutes later . . .

Thank you so much for your speedy response. Unfortunately, I was the only one who witnessed this. She and I were in the classroom with six children. Both the teacher I work with and my supervisor were out for the day. However, I immediately let the teacher know through text message. I notified my supervisor of the occurrence as soon as I got to work the following morning. There are currently plans to terminate her from the job. Would this change plans to notice?

[Not really, she could move to another job.]

I also wrote a detailed email to my supervisor outlining the events and the timeline of that morning. I also attached the screenshot of the text to my co-teacher.

##

You mentioned his lips were blue, did you take him to the school nurse? Did she create an incident report? Is the child verbal and a reliable witness? Were there any bruises? If any of this is the case perhaps the child and/or the nurse could be the witness and describe what happened. Were the parents informed? What was their reaction?

You certainly can file a Notice against the person, but the Board is likely to look at it as a she-said/she-said situation. If you handle it informally, perhaps the person will explain why she did what she did or possibly apologize profusely. If she outright denies it happened, you do not have much recourse.

##

Five minutes later . . .

We do not have a school nurse on staff as we are a charter school with a tight budget. He is verbal; however, he wouldn't be able to state what happened to him. His parents were informed and the mother was very upset. The mother told my supervisor that if this BCBA is allowed back into the school she doesn't want her anywhere near him. This child has a history of health problems including issues with his heart and if she held him down for only a few seconds longer the outcome could have been much different.

I understand what you mean about the she said/she said and it's unfortunate that this could happen because I truly believe she shouldn't be in this field. I will consider my options but I suppose as of now I will wait to see what happens when she meets with my supervisor and management on Tuesday.

##

One final thought is it should be *you* talking to the BCBA, not your supervisor or anyone at corporate. You were the only witness and these others are operating on second-hand information. Do you know who informed the parents? Was that you?

The first-hand witness rule is firm.

##

Two minutes later . . .

I didn't feel that talking to the BCBA was the right step for me to take at that time. I am not certified by the BACB so I didn't think I was ethically obligated to speak to her about her behavior first. I am a teaching aide and without the lead teacher there or the supervisor I was afraid she would immediately make excuses for her behavior which she did without me having to say anything to her. She stated to me and a different teacher from another classroom, "I get scared when he cries because his lips turn blue" which is a lie. He gets blue when he can't breathe; such was the case when he developed croup a few months ago. She has a known history of slamming down those who accuse her of wrongdoing or making excuses for her behavior. This isn't the first time that she has acted aggressively towards children; this is just the first time I've seen it that it has been to this extent. My supervisor is also the one who notified the parents as she is the director of the school.

##

Actually, *anyone* can report a BCBA using the Notice form.

It would certainly appear that this BCBA acted inappropriately and likely paid the price for doing so. The writer/witness was urged to file a Notice even though the behavior analyst will most likely be fired since she could move to another job and repeat her dangerous reaction under similar circumstances. It is likely that this is not the first time that she responded this way to a client, and no one observed or reported the incident, which is unfortunate. First and foremost, we are responsible for the welfare of our clients and owe it to them to be vigilant in providing corrective feedback and conscientious action when the situation arises.

ETHICS QUESTION #35—RESPONSE FROM THE ETHICIST

Message to the Ethicist:
I wanted to see if something could be considered "more or least restrictive" in a scenario I encountered this week.

We have monthly fire drills for our office building, which houses a small ABA clinic. Most of our clients have behavioral issues that require exclusionary timeout for the safety of themselves and the staff. The clients are all very skilled at what to do when fire alarms go off and how to conduct themselves as long as staff are with them and able to model appropriate exiting.

This week, when we had a fire drill, one of my clients was in seclusion . . . and was not ready to come out. She was engaging in a lot of physical aggression toward others when approached. We normally give her a few minutes until calm, then resume her schedule, and she is fine. However, the drill happened right after she went into seclusion. We then were faced with the dilemma of having to get her outside, as we were told by our company that this was something that was "non-negotiable."

Do you mean timeout?

> **Most likely what they meant to say was, "We are required to follow the instructions given to us by the fire department and the fire marshal and that, in order to keep our accreditation, we must present a warrant showing that we have followed all fire drills to the letter each and every time one occurs."**

I know that in a true emergency (which we knew this was not), we would do whatever it took to get the client(s) out of the building to safety, unless unable to do so. I also know that due to my learning history with this client that the skill is in her repertoire, and she will follow directions to engage in fire drill behavior appropriately when not in seclusion.

> **But we must also comply with legal requirements of our setting and community, see Code 1.04 (d) below.**

1.04 Integrity [RBT]
1.04 (d) Behavior analysts' behavior conforms to the legal and ethical codes of the social and professional community of which they are members. (See also, 10.02a Timely Responding, Reporting, and Updating of Information Provided to the BACB).

However, that day, we had to do something with which I did not feel comfortable. We had to physically move a client that (according to the functional assessment) finds physical touch highly aversive. Because she would not put on her shoes, we had to pick her up and carry her outside with no shoes, and then bring her back into our building for the sake of a fire drill.

You really care about your client.

All this because we were told to. I don't think this falls into "least restrictive practice" and abuses our use of restraint and safety training unless warranted for the safety of the individual and staff. Am I on the right track here or completely off base?

I appreciate your insight in advance!

> **This may not be what you want to hear, but you should side with safety requirements in this case. Imagine a situation where you chose not to take her out of "seclusion" (was this really timeout?) because of the possibility that you might accidentally reinforce an inappropriate behavior. Later, if there was an actual fire and somehow this client was injured because she refused to leave, you could be considered responsible because of the incident several months prior. Safety concerns are higher on our priority list than behavior programs.**

While this writer should be applauded for her commitment to her client's well-being and in particular her concern with keeping the consistency and integrity of the behavior program, there are times when other laws, rules, values, and contingencies are simply more important. Behavior analysts are responsible for being aware of the laws of the local community where they work. This was one of those times.

ETHICS QUESTION #36—RESPONSE FROM THE ETHICIST

I have heard a lot of different opinions on an ethical question that I have, and I was wondering if you could help.

It is my understanding that companies cannot post pictures of their clients to social media or their websites. Ethical guideline 2.06 (e) mentions that we must not share any identifying information (written, photographic, or video) about current clients or supervisees within social media contexts.

This is correct. We feel that client confidentiality is very important. Some leeway is given if the photos are taken in such a way that the child's face is not visible. Here is Code 2.06 (e):

2.06 (e) Behavior analysts must not share or create situations likely to result in the sharing of any identifying information (written, photographic, or video) about current clients and supervisees within social media contexts.

This seems like a very clear indication that photos are not allowed to be shared.

Yes, this is correct; photos with any type of identifying information should not be shared.

However, I continue to see many companies posting pictures of their clients on social media and on their websites.

If this was instigated by a BCBA, the person can be reported by you.

I reached out to a behavior podcast and they gave me this response:

Thank you for talking about ethics in social media. As per our ethical guidelines (8.04), companies can post client photos to company website/social media accounts only if they do not use the client's first and last name and written consent for that specific purpose has been obtained.

2.06 (e) Maintaining Confidentiality *trumps* 8.04 (b), which actually pertains to presentations that an organization might present at a conference. It does not pertain to the marketing of a company.

This is correct.

For testimonials, 8.05 states that behavior analysts should not use testimonials from current clients.

If a testimonial . . . is used, a disclaimer should include that the client is a former client, whether it was solicited or unsolicited, and include an accurate description of the current relationship between the company and the testimonial (if there is a current one).

From a *former* client

This is very different from our previous guidelines (before January 2016). Many behavior analysis companies are slowly working on making sure their marketing meets the ethical guidelines.

This is a good course of action for every behavior analysis company.

Companies have the responsibility to work with their marketing teams to make sure that marketing is adhering to the ethical guidelines (even if marketing doesn't agree!).

Marketing does not drive ETHICS; it is the other way around.

Can a company post pictures of clients to social media/website as long as there is written consent and no identifying information?

NO. Just read 2.06 (e) and abide by the directions given there and you will be fine. Do not allow your marketing department to lead you astray.

Some companies are feeling commercial pressure to increase their visibility and compete in the marketplace despite the fact that most agencies have long waiting lists of clients and cannot serve all of those who desire ABA services. Many, as this question illustrates, believe that a marketing plan that uses adorable photos of camera-friendly clients and credible, enthusiastic testimonials from their parents will be their ticket to income growth and increased revenue flow. Such an approach is diametrically opposed to Code 2.06 (e) which requires strict control over information about clients' confidential information. This includes not showing the faces of the child clients. For more information on testimonials see Ethics Question #30.

ETHICS QUESTION #37—RESPONSE FROM THE ETHICIST

Good evening. I am reaching out for guidance regarding an ethical situation in which I am finding myself. I recently transitioned two clients onto my caseload from another BCBA that gave notice at our company. When I transitioned these clients and reviewed their cases, I found multiple ethical violations that had occurred.

Looking at the Ethics Code for reporting violations, my first course of action is to try and resolve the matter with that BCBA. I have reached out to review and discuss the violations; however, as the BCBA is no longer a part of our company and cannot remedy the situation, I am unsure what would be considered "resolved" in this case.

You are correct. This situation cannot be *resolved* at this point. Since the BCBA has left the company, your next step is to follow 7.02 (d) and determine if the violations meet the reporting requirements. If so, you can file a Notice with the BACB.

I greatly appreciate any guidance in this situation. Thank you in advance for your time and consideration.

##

Three days later from the BCBA who had the question . . .

I wanted to follow up on the situation to get a little more feedback. Thankfully, I have never found myself in a situation where I've had to report another BCBA as I've had the privilege of working with great, ethical practitioners. To provide more context, I'm inserting below the original email that I sent the BCBA.

Thank you for reaching out to try to get into contact with me. The reason that I have been reaching out to you has been to discuss the BACB PROFESSIONAL AND ETHICAL COMPLIANCE CODES. As a behavior analyst, it is my ethical responsibility to comply with the ethical code, and in this case, I am referring to code *7.0 Behavior Analysts' Ethical Responsibility to Colleagues*. As I have transitioned cases that were under your supervision, I have come across numerous ethical violations that I would like to bring to your attention. You will find my feedback below followed by the code items I believe have been violated.

Across the clients transferred to me, I came across programs that were implemented without signed consent, and behavior intervention programs were in place without a written behavior intervention program and signed consent. It also came to my attention that some of the signed programs were put into place immediately before the transfer of the case(s) rather than being in place since the onset of the program. I addressed this by immediately suspending the programs. I then created new, individualized written programming and presented this to receive signed consent from the parent.

Code 4.04—behavior analysis must obtain written approval of the behavior-change program before implementation;

Code 4.05—Describing Behavior Change Program Objectives—Behavior analysts describe, in writing, the objectives of the behavior-change program to the client before attempting to implement the program.

I also noticed a program that I had specifically created/written for another client on my caseload and that this program had been introduced by you on this case without making any changes to the program. The program even had the wrong pronouns. For example, it said "he will" for a female client instead of "she will" and the target behaviors were written specifically for the original client's family structure. We all collaborate and share great ideas for all our clients; however, programs need to be individualized to each client. I addressed this by modifying the program to fit the client's needs and goals.

Code 4.03 Individualized Behavior-Change Programs
(a) Behavior analysts must tailor behavior-change programs to the unique behaviors, environmental variables, assessment results, and goals of each client;
(b) Behavior analysts do not plagiarize other professionals' behavior-change programs.

In addition, the clients had some programs that were not appropriate to the client, or were no longer needed. There was one program based off an assessment that was no longer appropriate for the client. In addition, program modifications were not made based on progress (or lack of) that was reflected with the data. I addressed this by modifying the programs to fit the client's needs and goals based on collected data and additional assessments.

(Code 3.01 Behavior-Analytic Assessment—(a) Behavior analysts conduct current assessments prior to making recommendations or developing behavior-change programs. The type of assessment used is determined by client's needs and consent, environmental parameters, and other contextual variables.)

I would still like to make sure we touch base and discuss the situations to ensure that this does not happen in the future. I am available to discuss these issues with you over the phone or set up a time to meet in-person with myself and my supervisor. Please let me know if you have any questions or if I need to clarify anything that I stated above. Thank you for your prompt attention to this matter.

Today, I was asked if this BCBA were to meet with me and provide a written statement that she has been made aware and will make sure she abides by the compliance code moving forward in her clinical practice, could that be considered "resolved." I thought this was an interesting point and was unsure so I'm looking for additional guidance on this matter.

##

Your email to the BCBA in question is very professional and exactly the sort of feedback that should be given under the circumstances. The Code is not clear as to how one might determine if there is a resolution of the problem. If the person raising the issue is satisfied, consider the Case closed. If not, then it is your option as to whether you wish to pursue it further by filing a Notice.

This BCBA handled a very difficult situation involving multiple ethical violations of a departing colleague. Not conducting current assessments, not obtaining prior approval for program changes, not describing objectives in advance, not individualizing the behavior-change programs and plagiarizing from other client programs are violations that are at the heart of what we are supposed to do as professional behavior analysts. This case also raises questions about the meaning of "resolution" when the careless BCBA is no longer around; this code item presumes that the person who needs feedback is still available to receive it. If the person has moved on, it may be up to the Code Compliance Committee to get involved once a Notice of Alleged Violation has been filed with the BACB.

ETHICS QUESTION #38—RESPONSE FROM THE ETHICIST

During the past three weeks, my boss . . . has been acting very unusual (extreme lethargy and not remembering conversations or events to the point where clients and parents have noticed). Parents have approached staff due to the concern that he has been under the influence while seeing and transporting their children.

Is he a BCBA?

Do you have contemporaneous notes indicating dates and times of these observations?

Today, I found a bottle of mixed pills (Vyvanse and Hydrocodone) prescribed to someone (who none of the staff have ever heard of) hidden in a child's wipe container. When staff requested a meeting, . . . our boss refused to meet until his attorney was available via phone.

BCBAs?

He claimed the pills belonged to a current client who is seen at 7pm by himself at the office. Our administrator for billing has never seen this name before.

Where do I go from here? Do I contact the police to have them discard the pills?

Who is holding the pills? If your boss is a BCBA, he is in violation of Code 1.05 (f) and he should submit a self-report of this incident to the Board. He could be reported via Notice of Alleged Violation to the Board if he is not responsive to your feedback on this issue. If he is not a BCBA, then it may be necessary to report him to some other authority. Is there a Board of directors of the company? If so, I would contact the chairman of the Board.

1.05 Professional and Scientific Relationships
(f) *Behavior analysts recognize that their personal problems and conflicts may interfere with their effectiveness. Behavior analysts refrain from providing services when their personal circumstances may compromise delivering services to the best of their abilities.*

The next day . . .

Thank you for your response. He is indeed a BCBA and yes, there is a paper trail of observations, etc.

Very good, make sure those are kept in a safe place.

Two of the staff who asked for the meeting were BCBAs and one was an RBT who has been working closely with him. The professionals were also concerned about his behavior.

Per his attorney's advice, the pills were flushed down the toilet and an incident report was written and signed. He is the owner of the company and there is not a Board of directors.

So, this is a private company with no oversight. This is not a good sign.

Also, I looked up the specific code and agree completely with him being in violation. I'll be sure to bring this to his attention (with a paper trail as well) to see if it can be resolved before reporting to the Board.

Based on the description of his behavior, it sounds like this company owner may need to take some time off and possibly go into treatment. Would there be a second-in-command who could take over if he needs to take a leave of absence?

Ten months later in response to my question about the outcome . . .

I left the company as his behaviors did not improve. As far as I know, all of the contractors and administrative assistants I worked with at the company have left as well. His company is still in operation; however, most families have followed up with me or other BCBAs when we left because they were not comfortable staying with him. He was not reported.

Behavior analysts who abuse drugs or alcohol or develop an addiction that impairs their "ability to competently practice" must report this situation to the BACB within 30 days.[5] Failure to do so is a violation of the Code of Ethics 10.02 (c) and certain sanctions may apply. All of us working in the field, and representing the profession, must be constantly aware of impressions we make on our clients and other professionals. First and foremost, we have an obligation to protect our clients from harm especially if it should occur due to our own personal failings. Under 7.02 (b) of the Code, behavior analysts are required to be aware of the potential of harm to clients and " . . . take the necessary action to protect the client . . . "

ETHICS QUESTION #39—RESPONSE FROM THE ETHICIST

I work in the Middle East and people here love giving gifts/food (e.g. when professionals such as behavior analysts go to a home session, the parents will often bring out elaborate food/snacks, etc.)

This is a slippery slope.

I'm just wondering how this fits with the BACB Ethics Code item 1.06 (d), "Behavior analysts do not accept any gifts from or give any gifts to clients because this constitutes a multiple relationship . . ."

Yes, this is correct, according to our Code of Ethics. Accepting food is a form of gifting and should be politely refused.

and Code 7.01 which says, "Behavior analysts promote an ethical culture in their work environments and make others aware of this Code."

Certainly Code 7.01 comes into play here as well since "ethical culture" includes educating all employees, and clearly all behavior analysts, about all aspects of the Code of Ethics and the rationale behind each element.

I work in a center where we provide ABA services to children. We have therapists who primarily deliver 1:1 ABA services. Most of these therapists don't have credentials from the BACB and let's say they are not planning to become certified in the near future.

Is there some reason for this?

We have supervisors who are BCBAs and they oversee the cases.

The supervisors are responsible for the cases even though the therapists are not RBTs.

Actually, no.

Does this "not receiving gifts" code apply to the frontline therapist even if they are not certified by the Board?

Or does the BCBA have the ethical responsibility to promote this "not receiving gifts" to the frontline staff?

Under Code 7.01, as you described above, behavior analysts are obligated to "promote an ethical culture" including politely refusing a gift of food. In this case the BCBA should educate the frontline staff about the perils of becoming friends with the families of clients (i.e. exchanging gifts). This will often turn out badly. The BCBA does have authority over the line staff and could require them to refuse food gifts from parents of the clients under 1.06 (d).

Promoting an ethical culture is a sizable task but is certainly an appropriate goal for professionals in our field. There are so many contingencies that wear away at our value system and Code of Ethics that we all have to be vigilant every working day. A frontline staff member who accepts a gift may feel it is necessary to offer a gift in the future or to grant a favor to the client. Becoming overly friendly with parents or caregivers can lead to a drift in the relationship and a decline in the integrity of treatment which will impact the child client directly in a negative way. The ideal relationship with parents and caregivers is one of being friendly but not friends and is a narrow path that behavior analysts have to navigate daily. When the initial contract for services is signed, it is a good time to have the parents sign a "Declaration" which includes rules for behavior analysts who are visiting homes.

ETHICS QUESTION #40—RESPONSE FROM THE ETHICIST

As a behavior analyst, I am deeply invested in the implementation of evidence-based practices with roots in ABA. As an administrator for a school district, I have recently become immersed in a situation for which I'd love to receive your input.

Oh, no, not again!

In my little area of California, there has been a surge of families that are embracing Rapid Prompting Method (RPM) and Spelling to Communicate (S2C).

Have you been in touch with CalABA about this? They are well connected in the state and would be in a position to try and educate the public about this.

As an outside observer, the premise of RPM and S2C look reminiscent of the Facilitated Communication days with the exception being that now the "communication partner" is holding the spelling board rather than touching the student.

They are basically the same.

In our community, parents have initially implemented RPM and S2C in the home, but in more recent weeks, I'm learning of requests to train school staff to implement these techniques and now, I've received a parent request for their child to receive cognitive/achievement testing with a "communication partner." We have no simple way of identifying whether it is the child or communication partner responding to the questions on the standardized test.

Behavioral staff should refuse to participate in the implementation of these non-behavior analytic interventions since this is not permitted under Code 8.01 (b).

8.01 Avoiding False or Deceptive Statements [RBT]
8.01 (b) Behavior analysts do not implement non-behavior-analytic interventions. Non-behavior-analytic services may only be provided within the context of non-behavior-analytic education, formal training, and credentialing. Such services must be clearly distinguished from their behavior-analytic practices and BACB certification by using the following disclaimer: "These interventions are not behavior-analytic in nature and are not covered by my BACB credential." The disclaimer should be placed alongside the names and descriptions of all non-behavior-analytic interventions.

Actually, there are some simple ways of doing this. If you can get a copy of the PBS documentary DVD *Prisoners of Silence*, there is a demonstration of how this is done.

In my town, there is even a nonpublic school hoping to open in the fall touting these principles.

I'm reaching out to you because I'm curious if ABAI will be taking a more visible stance regarding RPM/S2C practices and the potential harmful effects of implementation. In compiling information to best prepare myself for parent requests, I found ABAI's 1995 Statement on Facilitated Communication. I'm extremely hopeful that ABAI is considering taking a similar stance on RPM/S2C and if so, if there is a task force currently looking into this more.

To find out if there is any action on this issue, contact someone on the Board of directors of ABAI. They can tell you if ABAI plans to take any action.

Facilitated Communication and its offspring, Rapid Prompting, has a long and sordid history going back to the 1980s. These procedures are almost universally recognized as pseudoscience that can have damaging consequences for clients and their caregivers. Behavior analysts should be very aware that despite numerous published research studies debunking FC, this non-evidence-based approach will just not go away and that they will sometimes be pushed to incorporate it into legitimate behavioral treatment strategies by parents or teachers.

A very good reference on this is: Todd (2015). Also note that the American Speech-Language-Hearing Association (ASHA) now, officially discourages the use of Facilitated Communication and the Rapid Prompting method as "baseless practices" that could cause harm. Go to: www.asha.org/policy/ps2018-00351/ for details.

ETHICS QUESTION #41—RESPONSE FROM THE ETHICIST

I was approached by a student today whose employer has a policy that requires that *all* publications/ conference presentations by the student both be approved by the company administration *and* include the name of the company as the student's primary affiliation. This is irrespective of if the work is done on company paid time or uses the resources of the company. In addition, the company requires the student to present their proposed talk to the administrators of the company before going to the conference to present it, and the administrator has the right to disapprove the presentation or make changes.

> **This "policy" would not stand unless it was in a contract that the student signed. This is a classic example of an owner, a BCBA-D no less, exploiting a student by requiring her to sign a contract that violates Code 1.07 (a).**

1.07 Exploitative Relationships [RBT]
(a) *Behavior analysts do not exploit persons over whom they have supervisory, evaluative, or other authority such as students, supervisees, employees, research participants, and clients.*

While I am unaware of anything specific to this question in "The Code," I see this situation as being similar to the section dealing with authorship where in this case, having a supervisor who was not involved in a project insisting that his or her name and affiliation be on a publication or presentation.

> **The relevant Code here is Code 9.08 on acknowledging contributions by others.**

9.08 Acknowledging Contributions
Behavior analysts acknowledge the contributions of others to research by including them as co-authors or footnoting their contributions. Principal authorship and other publication credits accurately reflect the relative scientific or professional contributions of the individuals involved, regardless of their relative status. Minor contributions to the research or to the writing for publications are appropriately acknowledged, such as in a footnote or introductory statement.

> **In addition, the APA Code of Ethics has similar language.**

8.12 Publication Credit[6]
(a) *Psychologists take responsibility and credit, including authorship credit, only for work they have actually performed or to which they have substantially contributed. (See also Standard 8.12b, Publication Credit.)*
(b) *Principal authorship and other publication credits accurately reflect the relative scientific or professional contributions of the individuals involved, regardless of their relative status. Mere possession of an institutional position, such as department chair, does not justify authorship credit. Minor contributions to the research or to the writing for publications are acknowledged appropriately, such as in footnotes or in an introductory statement.*

Finally, the company has a policy that establishes anything done by the employee becomes the "intellectual property" of the company. It doesn't matter if this is done on paid time or the employee's own time.

> **This would not even pass the smell-test, no company can claim control over work done on an employee's own time with their own resources.**

The point here is that we have many students who conduct research as part of their graduate training and outside the scope of their employment.

> **Yes, a good percentage of students conduct research projects outside of their place of employment.**

In my opinion, the products of student/employee work completed under the supervision of their academic advisor should *not* somehow automatically be claimed as the property of the company.

Being an employee does not give the employer the right to claim ownership of the work of the student/employee 24/7.

This is correct.

Correct.

Requiring students to use the affiliation of their place of employment if their research is published does not match the BCBA Code of Ethics nor the APA Code. Students' work completed while enrolled at a university for a thesis or dissertation requires that they use the university as their affiliation; this is the case even if it is published after they have graduated. The general rule is that affiliation credit is given where the work was done and the same rule should apply to a company where the student works while in school. If the work was done with company resources on company time, then the company should also be given credit. The opposite is also true; if done on the student's time away from a company site and with their own resources, then no credit is given to the company.

ETHICS QUESTION #42—RESPONSE FROM THE ETHICIST

I am an ABA therapist working with children with ASD in Europe. I am contacting you as I have an ethical issue related to my professional practice.

I was contacted recently by the mother of a child I worked with for a few years as a home-based therapist. The family moved to the US a few months ago. The mother just informed me that she and the father are currently in the process of divorce. The father requests 50–50 custody over the child, but she would like to limit his custody to a minimum, as she believes he cannot fully assume his role as a father and an educator of a child with autism. The mother believes that the father might compromise their child's ABA therapy as he has always shown to be reluctant to ABA and to the suggestions made by different professionals.

The mother asked me, as well as other therapists who have worked with the child, to write a document sharing our observations about the role each parent played during the years we worked with the family. She hopes that this letter might speak in her favor to get custody.

As a general rule, it is not a good idea to get involved in a custody battle.

I think a diplomatic way in this situation is to write a document which aims to provide my observations about the progress the child made during the years of ABA therapy he received and to recommend the implementation of this approach in the future, without going into specifics about the parents and defending the position of one parent.

The approach you have described sounds reasonable. Keep in mind that we are behavior analysts and that we are an evidence-based field; we do not make broad projections or provide a prognosis based on our data, we leave this to PhD clinical psychologists or marriage and family therapists or developmental psychologists. Another approach is to say, "I'm sorry I don't feel comfortable preparing a document about this since I do not know what will happen in the US following this divorce." But, back to your original idea, you could prepare a carefully written document based on the child's progress. Keep in mind your obligations under 1.04, 2.04 (b), and 2.10 of the Code of Ethics.

2.04 (b) If there is a foreseeable risk of behavior analysts being called upon to perform conflicting roles because of the involvement of a third party, behavior analysts clarify the nature and direction of their responsibilities, keep all parties appropriately informed as matters develop, and resolve the situation in accordance with this Code.

The next step will be to communicate this document to the relevant party. The mother asked me to send it to the forensic psychologist she hired and to her lawyer.

The third-party in this scenario is the forensic psychologist and lawyer.
If you do prepare a report, it needs to be sent to the father as well since he has 50% custody. If you do not share reports with the father, his attorney can subpoena them through the court.

I am not sure how to proceed in this situation. I am afraid that sending them the document will automatically mean that I defend the mother's position and it would force me to respond to any additional questions they may have.

Keep your report neutral and data-based. Basically, what you are saying is that when behavioral procedures are used in this way they are effective and here are my data to prove that. You should say nothing about either parent.

As I have never been confronted with this kind of situation as a therapist, I need some advice about what would be the appropriate way to respond in respect to the behavior analysts' ethical code.

This is a prime case of a behavior analyst being called on to " . . . *perform conflicting roles because of the involvement of a third party* . . . " In almost all cases the behavior analyst is not properly trained or credentialed to negotiate the boiling waters of a divorce without putting themselves at risk for wading into opposing currents which could have serious implications for the behavior analyst's future practice. The best rule is to stay out of custody battles and let the parents hire other professionals who deal with custody issues on a regular basis.

ETHICS QUESTION #43—RESPONSE FROM THE ETHICIST

I have a question regarding the use of ABA client photos on company webpages. Specifically, I learned in my graduate studies for ABA that client photos could never be used on a webpage as this is a violation of confidentiality. In the code, there seems to be two recommendations regarding this. One, Code 8.04 (b), implies that identifying information be withheld from electronic media UNLESS consent is obtained.

8.04 (b) Behavior analysts making public statements or delivering presentations using electronic media do not disclose personally identifiable information concerning their clients, supervisees, students, research participants, or other recipients of their services that they obtained during the course of their work, unless written consent has been obtained.

This Code item pertains to public presentations at conference. If you are going to discuss a study at a conference you would need to: a) disguise the information in such a way that members of the audience would not be able to identify where the study was conducted or anyone participating in the study, and b) before you give this presentation, you need consent from anyone whose information does appear in the slideshow, e.g. the name of the facility, the names of the research assistants or of clients. This Code item does not imply that with consent you can allow identifiable client information to creep into your talk and it certainly does not imply that you can use a photo of the client since that would be a violation of Code 2.06 (a).

Code 8.04 (c), however, requires obscuring identifying information whenever possible.

8.04 Media Presentations and Media-Based Services
8.04 (c) Behavior analysts delivering presentations using electronic media disguise confidential information concerning participants, whenever possible, so that they are not individually identifiable to others and so that discussions do not cause harm to identifiable participants.

Note that this Code item clarifies that identifying information such as a photo is not allowed in conference presentations. It is clear that 8.04 (c) supersedes 8.04 (b).

It is clearly an ethical violation to use client photos on a webpage *without* client consent.

Yes, or in a presentation *or* photos in the hallway of their agency.

My question is, what about using client photos *if consent has been obtained* to display them on a webpage or in the hallway of an agency?

No, the client is entitled to their right of confidentiality and this cannot be given away even by the parents. Code 2.06 (a) is applicable in these situations.

2.06 Maintaining Confidentiality RBT
(a) Behavior analysts have a primary obligation and take reasonable precautions to protect the confidentiality of those with whom they work or consult, recognizing that confidentiality may be established by law, organizational rules, or professional or scientific relationships.

Is the use of client photos on the web, even with consent for their use, a violation of the BACB Ethics Code?

Since they are covered by the Code, behavior analysts should not request permission from parents to post photos of their child clients. Doing so would allow anyone to discover

that the child has a special diagnosis and is undergoing behavioral treatment. Child predators on the web or service delivery personnel who visit a clinic or private school for developmentally delayed children could identify the clients from looking at photos. Parents should be discouraged from giving away information about their children.

This question is extremely important in that it touches at the heart of an important issue for everyone in our field. It is clear that we are working with vulnerable populations, whose diagnosis of ASD, ID, or DD puts them at risk of discrimination at best and cruel bullying or even sexual assault by adults who mean them harm.[7] This from an NPR yearlong investigation using Justice Department data on sex crimes: "The results show that people with intellectual disabilities— women and men—are the victims of sexual assaults at rates more than seven times those for people without disabilities." Obviously, the more their vulnerabilities are exposed (such as by identifying them by name or photo), the greater they are at risk. Photos in the hallway or offices of a treatment facility are seen by some as a way of appearing consumer friendly but the bottom line is that the intention is to draw in more business. There is no payoff to the client and parents may think that by giving consent, their child will receive some extra benefit or special treatment. This is short sighted given the exposure to the general public which may include predators.

ETHICS QUESTION #44—RESPONSE FROM THE ETHICIST

I was informed by the principal of local private school that serves children with special needs that she was presented with an offer by a high-ranking individual from a major southern-city-based behavior analysis company. She stated that this individual offered her an amount of money for each child that she (or anyone else at the school) refers to receive behavioral services from their company in exchange for only allowing this company's therapists into the school.

> **This is a clear violation of 2.14 of our Code of Ethics. We take a "no kickbacks" position on such business arrangements since they are dishonest and work to the disadvantage of the clients.**

2.14 Referrals and Fees
Behavior analysts must not receive or provide money, gifts, or other enticements for any professional referrals. Referrals should include multiple options and be made based on objective determination of the client need and subsequent alignment with the repertoire of the referee. When providing or receiving a referral, the extent of any relationship between the two parties is disclosed to the client.

She stated to me that she was greatly offended by this offer and that she told this person she would in no way tell companies who are helping her other students that they could no longer provide immensely beneficial ABA services to her other students because of this agreement.

> **Good response. You should encourage her to report this person to the Board.**

Secondary to this offer, this person stated that this agreement is something that has been accepted at other schools.

> **So, if there are unethical people out there who have accepted this offer, if they are known, and there is documentation, they can be reported too.**

This tells me that it is possible that a child receiving services with another ABA company cannot be observed or treated for any socially significant behavioral issues or deficits in their school setting by anyone else other than those at a particular company.

In turn, when probing for barriers to entering schools to do behavior analysis consulting, my fellow colleagues said they had actually been denied access to other schools and which stated they "couldn't let them in."

> **This should be looked into but it would have to be one of your "fellow colleagues" since they would have first-hand knowledge of this type of violation.**

Or at least exploitation: Code 1.07.

In my honest opinion, this raises a massive issue for the ABA community in my state, the field of ABA in general and most importantly, the clients. Not only is this a bribe by this company representative but, this also results in what I believe is possible coercion in the form of telling parents.

If you want your child's services at the school (which happens often) then you must go to this company or change companies regardless of effectiveness.

What can be done about this?

> **The Code requires those with first-hand information to file the Notice against the individual behavior analyst who is behind this.**

What makes this situation unethical and offensive is the offer of a pay-out for only allowing the company's therapists in the school. The BACB Professional and Ethical Compliance Codes for Behavior Analysts assumes that behavior analysts are honest, law-abiding citizens who are straightforward in their dealings with clients and the public (as spelled out in 1.04 Integrity) and this sort of underhanded, unscrupulous conduct is simply not acceptable. Honest behavior analysts must realize that they have a duty-bound honor to assist in policing the field to detect and report this sort of reprehensible conduct that attaches a stigma to us all.

ETHICS QUESTION #45—RESPONSE FROM THE ETHICIST

I have a colleague who is a BCBA and she is part owner of an ABA service provider company. She does not use her real name on Facebook, but she does list BCBA as her credential and lists her job as manager of the ABA service provider (with the name attached).

> **Are you saying she lists a fake name with BCBA behind it? This is certainly a misrepresentation if she is doing this.**

Yesterday, she responded to another student's Facebook post about an FDA position on vaccines by saying (I'm summarizing) that she believes vaccines cause autism and are a conspiracy by big pharma, so she does not vaccinate her child. She further suggested that the only way to know for sure if vaccines cause autism is for everyone to stop vaccinating for five years to see if overall prevalence rates of autism decrease.

I'm concerned that she is advocating her anti-vaccination stance to the families and staff members with whom she works. I'm further concerned because as a colleague, she not only represents the field of applied behavior analysis, but also the educational program where I work. Further, her organization provides a training site for BCBAs coming through the ABA program at my school. If she is advocating this position, she has a wide audience.

A lot of people could report her.

My question is: What steps (if any) should I take? Is this a reportable offense?

> **Yes, it is a clear violation of 8.01 (a).**

8.01 Avoiding False or Deceptive Statements RBT

(a) *Behavior analysts do not make public statements that are false, deceptive, misleading, exaggerated, or fraudulent, either because of what they state, convey, or suggest or because of what they omit, concerning their research, practice, or other work activities or those of persons or organizations with which they are affiliated. Behavior analysts claim as credentials for their behavior-analytic work, only degrees that were primarily or exclusively behavior-analytic in content.*

Do what is right for the field.

It's likely that if I do report and she loses her license (I don't know if this could happen or is likely), she will also lose her livelihood and she is a new parent.

Students at my program will also suffer as they're accruing BCBA hours through her organization.

> **Hopefully, your students can read the latest research about vaccines and make wise decisions about where they choose to work.**

I'm not sure what to do and would appreciate any guidance you can provide.

> **The right thing to do is to report this to the Board via Notice of Alleged Violation. If the BCBA influences people with bogus information, their children and other children could suffer horribly. Here is a link that provides the proper information.[8]**

Behavior analysts are scientist-practitioners who support an evidence-based approach to treatment as well as the endeavors of the broader scientific community of academics and scholars who strive to rid the world of deadly diseases. As the article published in the *Journal of the American Medical Association* cited above makes clear, "*Parents who delay or skip childhood vaccinations even when kids have no medical reasons are contributing to U.S. outbreaks of measles and whooping cough.*" This BCBA is on record making, "public statements that are false, deceptive, misleading, exaggerated and fraudulent" and should be held accountable by our certification Board. It is unlikely that she will lose her certification or license but surely, she should be required to receive further education on the topic of vaccines and how promoting their refusal creates a risk of illness on a major community scale.

ETHICS QUESTION #46—RESPONSE FROM THE ETHICIST

I am an RBT. One of my supervisors has a client on her caseload who has engaged in noncompliance/tantrums/aggressions for the past year. These behaviors have increased in frequency and duration. While no formal data is taken . . .

This is a serious problem.

Data on something dangerous like this should be taken every day! This is required by Code 3.01 (b) . . .

3.01 (b) Behavior analysts have an obligation to collect and graphically display data, using behavior-analytic conventions, in a manner that allows for decisions and recommendations for behavior-change program development.

Is there data on this?

I would estimate that the client now spends 70% of his time at the clinic engaged in problem behavior. The BCBA *has never conducted a functional analysis* and no formal plan exists to respond to the problem behavior, despite the fact that I have asked for these things multiple times.

Do you have those requests in writing?

This is a clear violation of 3.01 (a) . . .

(a) *Behavior analysts conduct current assessments prior to making recommendations or developing behavior-change programs. The type of assessment used is determined by client's needs and consent, environmental parameters, and other contextual variables. When behavior analysts are developing a behavior-reduction program, they must first conduct a functional assessment.*

There is also no reinforcement system in place to proactively treat the problem behavior. The same demands are placed each day, and the child is expected to comply 100% of the time.

Not best practice.

The consequences delivered change almost daily, and often the BCBA or another RBT will physically hold the child in the chair. I refuse to do this.

Are the parents not complaining about this? What about the insurance company? What about the clinical director or the company owner?

I have taken this issue to the clinical director, who has agreed with me that it is wrong . . . but all she has done is agree to observe a session and make suggestions for the BCBA. She has expressed that because it is not her client, she cannot make decisions about the treatment plan.

This follows 7.02 (c).

This is not true, this is actually one of the *main* functions of the clinical director, to assure that treatment is humane, ethical, and effective.

I feel that this situation is highly unethical in multiple ways.

You are correct.

No assessments have been conducted other than an initial FBA that is a year old (and the child did not engage in noncompliance during the assessment). There is no formal plan to respond to the behavior, nor is any real data being taken and analyzed. I feel that holding the child in the chair is an unsafe consequence that is doing harm to the child. I have gone both to the BCBA and the clinical director, with no actions taken to improve the situation. At this point, I do not know what to do, and I am also afraid that I will lose my job if I report the situation.

You are correct. You could lose your job if you report this, but you have an ethical and moral obligation to see that something is done in this situation. Do you want to work for a company that is this unethical?

This BCBA's behavior is similar with all of her clients. Most of her data sheets are copied and pasted between clients, she does not supervise her RBTs or assess new problem behaviors, and most of her clients make limited progress.

If she copied programs and data sheets from someone else, this is plagiarism. If she has her own library of forms that she uses for "cookie cutter" programs, she is not providing the individualized treatment that clients deserve.

Do you have any advice for me?

This is certainly not best practice; in fact, it is a violation of 4.03 of the Code.

4.03 Individualized Behavior-Change Programs
(a) *Behavior analysts must tailor behavior-change programs to the unique behaviors, environmental variables, assessment results, and goals of each client.*
(b) *Behavior analysts do not plagiarize other professionals' behavior-change programs.*

Your next move is to look at the Notice of Alleged Violation form and see if you have sufficient evidence to report the BCBA and the clinical director, and simultaneously start looking for a position with an ethically operated company.

##

Two days later . . . from the behavior analyst.

Thank you for your quick response. I reviewed the Notice of Alleged Violation form, and I'm worried that I may not have sufficient evidence to report. The only request I have put in writing was on a supervisor's feedback form, which became part of the BCBA's personnel file. Additionally, I do not work directly with this client, so I do not have access to his treatment plans/data. Most of my information about the copying and pasting of treatment plans and lack of supervision/ongoing assessment and analysis comes from other RBTs, who are also afraid to report their concerns.

Only those with direct, first-hand knowledge may file a Notice, anything else is hearsay. It would fall to the RBTs to file the notice and since they come under the Code of Ethics they need to give this some consideration, by not doing anything they are condoning this unethical practice.

I am open to any suggestions you have going forward about how exactly to begin documenting these incidents.

Basically, any hard copies of documents that clearly show cut and pasting of names on behavior plans could be used as documentation and if there are any emails or memos directing the RBTs to engage in unethical practice, these would also count as evidence.

This is an unusual situation where the RBT on the team is more aware of the Code and best practices than the BCBA. She is aware that something is wrong with the execution of this treatment plan and had the wherewithal to take the issue to the clinical director *and* to contact the ABAI Hotline to ask for advice. In this case, it would appear that this outstanding RBT has exhausted all the available approaches and ordinarily would be justified in sending in a Notice of Alleged Violation except that she does not have first-hand information. For behavior analysts who are working in any setting, if you provide verbal feedback regarding ethical concerns, be sure to follow it up with something in writing so that you have a paper trail. And, while you may not have first-hand knowledge of significant violations, you can encourage those who do to take appropriate action.

ETHICS QUESTION #47—RESPONSE FROM THE ETHICIST

I work for a small private ABA clinic in the Southeast that is owned by a person who is trained both as a physical therapist (PT) and an occupational therapist (OT). She owns the ABA company and a separate company (that ABA shares a building with) that provides OT, PT, and speech and language therapy (SLT) services.

This looks complicated.

Does the ABA company have a BCBA as clinical director?

Many of the clients seen by the ABA company are also seen by the other clinic as well. Now, the owner also sees clients as an OT or PT (often OT for the ASD children).

Are the two companies physically separated and is there signage on each to indicate what they are?

My question/concern is as follows: Last week, a parent of a child I see (as a case supervisor) informed me that the owner, who has been providing OT therapy weekly, recommended a SIT (sensory integration therapy) procedure to manage the child's SIB.

You might have said something like, "Hmmm, I'm confused here, there really isn't any research showing that SIT is appropriate for self-injurious behavior, let me look into that and I'll get back to you . . ."

The problem is, while we try to help the clients understand that the two companies are distinct entities, many families are understandably unclear on this (given the same owner and office). While I had no issue recommending a behavior analytic intervention for the treatment of the SIB (a successful treatment had been provided several months earlier with resurgence recently occurring), I was left wondering how this is perceived by the client. On the one hand, the OT services are provided at the clinic while the ABA is provided in-home, but as an owner of an ABA program, the owner's recommendations could be fortified by her relation to ABA services.

So, 1) should I bring this concern to the owner . . .

Yes, use your best Dale Carnegie skills (Carnegie, 1981) and raise it as a question rather than an accusation; if the ABA company has a clinical director, it would be the job of that person to bring this up.

and, 2) as the owner of an ABA company, does our field's Code of Ethics apply to her?

Not if she is not a BCBA.

Is she responsible in an alternative clinical practice setting to adhere to her other company's requirements?

She would need to comply with the PT/OT Code of Ethics on this point. You could do some research on this to see if her code says anything about operating only within specified boundaries of competence and ethics.

Thank you in advance for your consideration.

##

One day later . . .

Thank you for your response. I shared your email with the clinical director (who I brought my concern to prior) and she will be speaking with the owner. To answer some of your questions:

1. The company does have a BCBA as a clinical director.
2. The ABA clinic shares a building with the OT, PT, and SLP services, although the door clearly states the name of both companies separately. Both have separate office phone numbers, tax IDs, LLCs, etc. (So they are legally separate entities.)
3. I did review the OT Code of Ethics the other day before emailing you. The only thing, as far as I can tell, related to evidence-based service provision is:
   1. "Use, **to the extent possible**, evaluation, planning, intervention techniques, assessments, and therapeutic equipment that are evidence based, current, and within the recognized scope of occupational therapy practice."

It seems, based upon the addition of the caveat I underlined and bolded above, that evidence-based practice is a strong *suggestion*, not a requirement, for the OT field.

Either way, I will send a follow-up email after the conversation occurs and let you know how she (as the owner) and we (as behavior analysts) choose to rectify or at least clarify practices going forward.

The next day . . .

The company owner, clinical director, and I met today to discuss the concern and possible solutions. Long story short, we agreed to a) provide a document delineating the distinction between the two clinics for client's receiving services from both including a description of services and contact information for senior-level staff and, b) if an OT/PT wishes to prescribe any intervention for a behavior concern for a client that is also seen by the ABA company, a team meeting will occur prior to the implementation of any treatment.

This is in keeping with 7.0 of the Code of Ethics.

7.0 Behavior Analysts' Ethical Responsibility to Colleagues
Behavior analysts work with colleagues within the profession of behavior analysis and from other professions and must be aware of these ethical obligations in all situations.

If the team wishes to pursue an alternative, non-behavioral intervention (e.g. SIT) that does not present any clear risk to the Client, the ABA team will assist in collection of intervention data.

This is in compliance with 2.09 (d).

2.09 Treatment/Intervention Efficacy
2.09 (d) Behavior analysts review and appraise the effects of any treatments about which they are aware that might impact the goals of the behavior-change program, and their possible impact on the behavior change program, to the extent possible.

Were you able to negotiate an agreement that if the data shows no effect of the "intervention" that they will agree to terminate and consider a behavioral approach instead?

Later that afternoon . . .

That specific language was not used. I did note that when implementing a behavioral procedure, we typically will wait approximately two weeks before revising should the child's behavior not show any improvement or desired effects. We also discussed the concern of using SIT procedures contingent upon the presence of a challenging behavior (e.g. deep pressure massage following physical aggression) and how this approach could have paradoxical effects, i.e. increasing the frequency of challenging behavior.

Lastly, I will be doing a training with the OT, PT, and SLP staff on behavior management practices and how BAs conceptualize and design behavior change treatment programs.

##

One day later . . .
    I just want to clarify that no ABA practitioner would implement a non-ABA treatment approach.

Very good. No *ethical* behavior analyst would implement a non-evidence-based treatment.

The OT and likely parents would implement the treatment approaches and the ABA staff would collect data on the targeted DV.

This could be a last resort if you are unable to convince the team to rely on evidence-based treatments.

Given this, would you proceed differently?

As a Plan B, take data as per 2.09 (d) to see what happens with the intervention/treatment but with the understanding that if it does not work the team and parents agree to go with an evidence-based treatment. They would need to agree, "We will try this out for 30 days and see what happens then revert to Plan A."

I was always led to believe that in these situations the ABA team could at least collect data to show whether or not the treatment is effecting changing in the child's behavior.

Yes, focus on collecting the data. It will be difficult to watch knowing that what you are seeing is taking up staff time and resources when those same resources could be used to improve the client's condition.

##

In response to my question a few weeks later, "Is there any follow up information you want me to include . . . "

Both clinics met and agreed that OT/PT would not make recommendations for managing behavior challenges without first consulting with the ABA clinic director for cases both groups work on.

##

Working with colleagues from another profession can be quite a challenge because they have a different theoretical background than we do about the origins and maintenance of behavior, they have quite different treatment strategies, do not insist on evidence-based methods to the extent that we do, and do not have the measurement tools to evaluate individual cases that we have. This case illustrates the complexities one can run into and the steps necessary to work them out amicably which is much more difficult than Code 7.0 suggests. The behavior analyst in this case worked hard to make sure that he was following our Code of Ethics while educating the owner of the two companies and their staff about necessary procedures in behavior analysis and protections against unethical conduct.

ETHICS QUESTION #48—RESPONSE FROM THE ETHICIST

I work for a school district and we are cleaning out our old files. The BCBA team is wondering if there are official guidelines for storing and destroying old data for exited students?

This question pertains to 2.07 of the Code, Maintaining Records.

(a) *Behavior analysts maintain appropriate confidentiality in creating, storing, accessing, transferring, and disposing of records under their control, whether these are written, automated, electronic, or in any other medium.*

(b) *Behavior analysts maintain and dispose of records in accordance with applicable laws, regulations, corporate policies, and organizational policies, and in a manner, that permits compliance with the requirements of this Code.*

We are curious about:

1. Storage (does it need to be in a locked file in a locked room)?

   There are ways that Personal Health Information (PHI) should be stored via federal HIPAA guidelines. Given that these are students of a public school, there are federal regulations that guide this process and some of those regulations are covered in the FERPA law (Federal Education Rights and Privacy Act) and IDEA (Individuals with Disabilities Education Act.

   So, FERPA is the federal student records law, and IDEA is the federal special education law. FERPA does not address how long records should be kept. School districts can establish their own policy and procedures. A standard is five to seven years after the student exits the educational program.

   IDEA requires only that certain records be created (e.g. evaluation reports, IEPs, etc.). IDEA does not set a time limit for maintaining documents. It does require schools to notify parents before records associated with special education are destroyed.

   Individual states often have their own student records laws that do dictate specific time frame for maintaining records. Your school administrators and IT department are a good place to help you get this information. Personal Health Information needs to be stored in a locked file in a locked room. For older hard copies, some facilities pay to have these records stored at an off-site facility for healthcare documents (HIPAA compliant). There are other best practices for storing confidential data including restricting access and appointing one person in charge of the files.

2. What needs to be in a client file?

   Because there are both federal requirements and requirements an individual school district may have, check with a school administrator on this.

3. How long to keep a file?

   A good rule for behavioral records is seven years. School transcripts must be kept much longer.

4. How do you destroy the file?

Typically, larger agencies hire a service that shreds confidential information. The service provides a certificate that confirms that those documents were properly destroyed.

5. How do we keep e-data secure?

This is a question for the IT person and/or administrator in your school or district. Be aware that not all cloud storage is HIPAA compliant.

Code 2.07 establishes the standards for records maintenance and disposal that are expected of behavior analysts but as you can see there are no details on how to accomplish this goal. The authors wish to thank Devon Sundberg, CEO of Behavior Analysis Center for Autism, for her expert assistance in responding to this question.

ETHICS QUESTION #49—RESPONSE FROM THE ETHICIST

Message

One of my workers referred her friend's child to me.

> This could be a dual relationship.

Are you a solo provider or do you work for a company? If a company, they may have a policy on required cleanliness of home settings before staff may work there.

I was going to accept the case and not have the employee who is a friend on the case. I set up an evaluation and met the family at the house. The mother was very nice. The issue I had is it was difficult to walk up the stairs because of clutter on the stairs. There was long box halfway up the stairs but there was a small path I could maneuver around. There were other things on the stairs as well. I felt some parts of the house were not clean (crumbs next to me on the table in the house, dusty things). The children did NOT appear to be in danger at all from the unkempt house and they were clean. I just knew right away we could not do home-based therapy in the house due to OSHA laws but it made the evaluation a little awkward.

Therapists should not have to work in a dirty, cluttered, possibly unsafe environment.

I didn't feel comfortable navigating their house so I mainly observed the three-year-old boy with an ASD diagnosis. Usually if the child feels comfortable, I try to play and interact and have a fun time to make the evaluation exciting. I had the mom sign the consent for the VB Mapp and the structured ABC assessment I was going to do. I explained to her that I was going to mostly observe to figure out why the aggressive behaviors are occurring and to do the VB Mapp assessment. I told the mother to just go about what they normally do. I told her it may be a little awkward but I need a good picture of what is going on. The child I was observing had very flexible spontaneous language so I didn't think that I needed to do a lot of direct testing. I did ask him a few questions and he would politely decline to answer. I didn't want to push him on the first day of meeting him so I didn't ask too many questions. Also, his deficits are not language related; they are in the areas of play skills and social skills so a lot of one-on-one direct testing was not warranted.

I also asked the mom questions from the AFLS home assessment. I learned that the child was aggressing on the family members at a high rate for attention. I am not sure if the mother liked hearing this information from me because she believed that maybe her son didn't realize what he was doing hurts people. She also said that they don't 100% believe the child has autism. I mentioned how autism can be different in each individual. I explained my concern over the boy's leisure and play skills and how children his age usually find things on their own to play with. The mother said that most children his age need a lot of direction on play activities. The mother seems in semi-denial.

> This is starting to look like lack of interest or buy-in.

I told the mother that due to the boy's aggression, which is mainly targeted at his sister, it may be easier if we do sessions at a preschool or daycare to work on play and social skills. Another option is teaching the sister how to respond differently so as not to reinforce him. At this time, I did not mention the home and the OSHA concerns because the dynamic with the boy and his sister was enough to make me recommend doing therapy outside of the home. Also, the fact that he has social skills deficits warranted another location for therapy with peers. I can do some parent-and-sister training in the home to help decrease the aggression.

> This might be a good idea.

I tried to reach out to the mother after the evaluation but she seemed to be avoiding me for the next four days. I needed more intake forms signed and she wouldn't respond. (This was a lesson learned by me; all forms need to be signed prior to the evaluation.) The mother finally sent the forms at the end of the week. When I was leaving the house that day, the sister said she thought I would be playing with them. I have a feeling they were not happy with the evaluation because it was mostly observation, but I did the best I could with the condition of the home, the dynamics of the family, and the boy's attention-seeking aggression. I did my best to describe what I was going to do and my recommendations.

Mom said she was looking into the local school district as another option so I said to let me know what she thought about the district and to let me know if she would be sending him there rather than working with me. I said I would be happy to do some home parent training if they decide to go with the school system.

This is good, it gives you an out.

I guess I am asking, do I even mention the OSHA laws I need to follow?

My guess is the mom is very aware of her messy and possibly dangerous home (e.g. would she pass a fire marshal examination of exit routes in case of fire?), so I don't think that is necessary.

I am usually okay with giving feedback but I wouldn't want to insult someone the first time I met them.

Agreed.

You need to think through your autoclitics (Chapter 12 of Skinner's *Verbal Behavior*, The Autoclitic) and come up with a word combination that surfaces the issue but does not scare her away, e.g. "For in-home training, I will need a clear space to work with your son, would it be possible to move a few things . . .?"

I would take a couple of minutes to review Code items 4.06 and 4.07 prior to pushing for the family to become your client, I'm not sure the minimal conditions are there.

4.06 Describing Conditions for Behavior-Change Program Success
Behavior analysts describe to the client the environmental conditions that are necessary for the behavior-change program to be effective.

4.07 Environmental Conditions That Interfere With Implementation
(a) *If environmental conditions prevent implementation of a behavior-change program, behavior analysts recommend that other professional assistance (e.g., assessment, consultation or therapeutic intervention by other professionals) be sought.*
(b) *If environmental conditions hinder implementation of the behavior-change program, behavior analysts seek to eliminate the environmental constraints, or identify in writing the obstacles to doing so.*

And, back to the relationship between the potential client and your employee, that is in the gray area of multiple relationships. While it does not seem to be close, there is a good chance that the worker will want to talk to you about it, "Hey, how's it going with Timmy? I heard the mom is not really happy with you . . ."

The cleanest solution is to let this mother work with the school district. If she comes back to you voluntarily, then you can refer her to some other agency. If you do accept this case, you will have to decide if you are willing to deal with the cleanliness/messiness issue. Crumbs on a table can be brushed off. The bigger concern is being unable to navigate around the house to work with the child.

##

Two hours later . . .

Thank you so much for your input. I am a solo provider and didn't really think about the multiple relationship when I accepted. I am not going to push for this family to work with me, and they will most likely choose to work with the school.

##

The focus of the BCBA in this case is on whether her RBTs would be willing to work in a home that is so dirty and unkempt. My interpretation of 4.06 and 4.07 is that the environment where behavior analysts conduct therapy needs to be orderly and hygienic with few distractions. In addition, one of the *environmental conditions that are necessary for the behavior-change program to be effective* includes full cooperation on the part of the parent. This mother does not seem to be convinced that her son really needs help or that he is autistic. These are not ideal circumstances under which to start a behavior program.

ETHICS QUESTION #50—RESPONSE FROM THE ETHICIST

I live in Dubai and I have been a behavioral therapist since 2011. I am an RBT and I have started my BCBA course, in which I am learning about Ethics in Applied Behavior Analysis. As I read through the core principles of Ethics, I can see that my supervisor doesn't follow the Ethics Code. I believe I should report some of the issues below.

Specifically, I provide home-based services and I often see my clients getting slapped in the face by their parents. In fact, one day when I went for the session, my six-year-old client pointed to the marks on his face and reported that his mother hit him. When I confronted the mother, she immediately confessed saying that she is fed up with the child not listening to her. I discussed the entire situation with my supervisor who didn't seem to be taking any action. When the parents came for the review session with my supervisor, the mother slapped the child in front of my supervisor, and the child yelled and jumped from his chair. My supervisor did not bother to look into this.

5.01 assumes that the supervisor is competent to handle these situations.

Has your supervisor observed you, in person working with this family in their home? Has your BCBA supervisor conducted a FA for this child? Are you implementing a compliance program with this child?

I have emails to document that I also reported to my supervisors another client who is 11-years old and both of her parents hit her frequently. She sometimes screams during our sessions, "I DONT WANT TO GO TO CORNER." Her mother reported to me proudly, "I gave her a slap because she passed urine in her bed." All of this was reported to my supervisor via my emails and she did not bother to take any action.

Weak, ineffective supervisor.

It became very difficult to help the child as her problem behaviors were increasing during the sessions. She would scream and would be extremely afraid if her mother came close to her. With no help provided by the supervisor for this particular case, I had to refer the client to my supervisor.

Then what happened?

When my clients are engaging in disruptive behaviors, I often ask my supervisor to help me with a plan to help the child, but there is no response.

So, your "supervisor" has not visited the home and has not conducted a FA.

She expects us to come up with our own consequences and is not even bothered by the problems. She says that we all manage disruptive behaviors which is right on her part but I am an RBT who should be given guidelines by a BCBA as to how to change the child's behavior.

RBTs need behavior plans.

Parents often express their distress to me that my supervisor is not cooperative, she does not arrange a review meeting to discuss the child's progress, and she is not sending the latest program for working with the child.

Do you think the parents would be willing to file a Notice of Alleged Violation with the BACB? This would most likely get the supervisor's attention.

The centers providing ABA services are not as large as they are in the United States so clients have to depend on services that are available.

Does your supervisor have a boss? Did your supervisor sit with you and describe what this supervision experience would be like at the beginning? Have you read section 5.0 of the Code of Ethics lately? This tells you exactly how you should be treated as a supervisee.

##

One week later . . .

Let me start from the beginning. Six years ago, my supervisor got certified and I was the first one who started working with her. She would assign me cases and I went to client homes to provide therapy. As my supervisor was establishing in her career as a BCBA, she started training a lot of people and giving out certificates showing completion of ABA training. When the Board started certifying therapists as RBTs, my supervisor started extensively training a countless people to earn a bundle of money. Two years ago, she started a center with over 30 staff working at the center and more than 30 therapists providing home-based therapies. There are at least 80–100 children attending the center and she is responsible for supervising all the therapists and creating programs for all of the children.

This doesn't seem possible.

This clearly looks like a violation of 5.02. If you look at the BACB Applied Behavior Analysis Treatment of Autism Spectrum Disorder: Practice Guidelines for Healthcare Funders and Managers, p. 35, the maximum with the "support of one BCaBA is 24."

For every review session (therapist and clients meet with the BCBA) she charges the parent *and* RBT also for acquiring RBT supervision hours.

This is a violation of 1.04 and 2.12 (c) of the Code of Ethics and may be billing fraud.

This BCBA is not doing just one but many things that appear to be unethical.

1. She trains new people to become RBTs but she does not provide ongoing staff training despite staff requesting this, multiple times. She repeatedly tells the staff, "You have to tell me what you want training on," we do, and then she never provides it.
2. After the review with the parent, the supervisor is supposed to send an updated program for me to use when working with the client. This program doesn't come for weeks and sometimes months and clients keep asking me, "Why hasn't your supervisor sent new goals?" I keep maintaining old targets with my clients.
3. When my clients offer me gifts I refuse explaining I am not allowed to accept gifts. Three weeks ago, when I was at the center, one of the clients (a child's parent) came in with a few special treats from her hometown and offered them to me and my supervisor. I looked at my supervisor and said, "We are not allowed to accept this." To this, she said, "No, it's okay, you can take it," and she herself accepted a few and remarked, "This client is my former student, I trained her for becoming an RBT so you can take treats from her." I was confused!
4. One of my clients started showing disruptive behaviors in school by hitting and scratching teachers and the shadow teacher (learning support assistance). The mother was very worried and this was reported to my supervisor via email from the school. I sent separate emails from my end as this behavior was escalating at home. Without making a school visit or recording any data, the supervisor completely relied on the ABC chart provided to her by the shadow teacher. She also made a BIP plan and sent it to the shadow teacher and school via email. After a week, the child's behavior got worse. The child started hitting herself and urinating in her bed and during the 1:1 session at home. She would hit anyone and scratch herself until she started to bleed. I reported to my supervisor that the child is not improving. The shadow teacher also constantly updated my supervisor that she is finding it difficult to manage the child's behavior at school. As of today, I have referred the child to my supervisor explaining that I cannot work with the client as she has started showing a lot of disruptive behaviors. I thought this was best for myself as I am getting NO HELP from my supervisor and I was in a dilemma about why my supervisor is not doing anything about this. I was feeling very guilty of not being able to help that child who is suffering so much. Her parents are hitting her all the time in front of me (this is the girl I referred to in my previous email).
5. My supervisor currently owns two centers. She is her own boss and supervises more than 60 therapists and creates programs for more than 80 children.
6. In Dubai, there are very few providers of ABA services and it is not easy to get a therapist who will provide home-based therapies. So, the clients would hesitate to file a complaint with the supervisor who would stop therapy for their child, causing them to have to go somewhere else for therapy.

7. None of Code 5.0 seem to be implemented by my BCBA since she wants to open more centers and earn more money. She might know she is practicing unethically but there is no one to check on her since she herself is the owner.

It would appear that this supervisor has been so engaged in growing her business that she has lost sight of the fundamentals of ABA and the proper management and cultivation of her supervisees. Expanding a business and generating more revenue can certainly be rewarding. The Code of Ethics, representing the values of the field, is intended to serve as a brake to contain the BCBAs enthusiasm and remind her of a fundamental commitment to clients and supervisees. In case you were not aware, there is a new law in Dubai, Federal Law No. 3, passed in 2016, also known as Wadeema's Law, that protects all children from any form of physical or psychological abuse; the parents should be reminded of this should you see any more slapping of their child. In this case, unless some containment is achieved, this single BCBA could significantly harm her clients and sully the reputation of behavior analysts and the field in this country for years to come.

ETHICS QUESTION #51—RESPONSE FROM THE ETHICIST

I recently gave a 30-day written notice to my employer due to unethical practices. I felt I could no longer continue to work for an unethical company.

> **Did you mention the unethical practices in your notice? Do you have a copy of that document?**

The company rejected my 30-days-notice, and instead gave me 10 minutes to pack up my belongings and leave the facility.

> **This is, sadly, fairly common now. Companies don't usually want someone around who might spread the word about the unethical conduct occurring there. There is also some concern that some employees may be vindictive and erase files, steal information, etc. if they are allowed to stay on the job for an extended period of time.**

All of my supporting documents of fraudulent paperwork is with my supervisors and the facility and I have no further access to this documentation.

Although I have documented several ethical code violations in my own record of dates and by whom, I do not have the actual documents to support my claims. Will the BACB look at my case even though I don't have the original documents to support these claims?

> **You can try to make the case to the Board, but they rely on documentation to prove a case against another behavior analyst. Is there anyone else who was an eyewitness to the unethical conduct who would be willing to provide a written, notarized statement?**

> **Depending on the severity of the ethical violations, and assuming you have documentation, you should send in a Notice.**

##

One day later . . .

Thank you so much for getting back with me so quickly. This is weighing heavily on me.

I am very hurt, and I'm trying not to let my emotions run this process.

I did not write anything about unethical conduct in my notice since I was afraid of what repercussions could come with that during the next several weeks of my employment with the company, but I do have a copy of the notice with the date of the notice and my last day.

When I decided I could no longer stay with the company, I thought I would have enough time to get copies of the documents I needed to support these claims. But, I was only given ten minutes to collect my belongings and was watched while doing so, I was unable to collect and copy those documents.

There are several RBTs and other employees who would write a statement in support of these claims. Three employees put their resignation notice within a matter of a couple weeks for reasons of unethical conduct. Out of the three, one voluntarily left the facility the day of. The other two, myself, and another RBT, were both told to leave.

> **You will need this documentation from them to support your Notice.**

1. In my contract and company handbook, the BCBAs are required to observe RBTs at least 5% of their hours in order to keep the RBT credential. I have not been supervised once during my three months of working at this company.

153

Instead, the BCBA has completed fraudulent paperwork claiming she has supervised me and made me sign it so, "We both reap the benefits": It looks as if she is completing her requirement, and I keep my RBT credential. I signed two of these papers before realizing it was fraudulent. *(You were exploited.)*

After realizing this was a problem, I started keeping an Excel document and writing down details of the papers given to me. All documents were brought to me to be signed and then were kept by supervisors. *(You should always request a copy.)*

I am not the only RBT that has never been observed but have claimed to be. There would be several people who would be willing to provide a written, notarized, statement of this. In addition, there are times and days on the document that would solely prove that the supervision hours were false. *(This is powerful evidence.)*

2. When hired through this company, I was aware of my three supervisors. To my knowledge, all supervisors were BCBAs and had the credentials to make programs for my clients that they supervised. After about two months of working at this company, I learned that a supervisor that the executive director had appointed was not a BCBA, nor an RBT, and has been making programs for my client. This person does not have the credentials to be making programs for any clients. This could cause harm to all clients she is supervising. All programs and documentations of this are in the client's file.

3. I gave a 30-days-notice to this company that I would be leaving. I could not ethically work for the company, but I wanted to give an appropriate amount of notice to help with transitions of my clients. *(This is a violation of the Code of Ethics.)* Thirty minutes after giving my notice to my supervising BCBA, I was approached in my room and told by the executive director/BCBA, "Since I hear you are so unhappy here, you will leave today." I had never met or talked to the executive director/BCBA until this date, and she came to me stating how I felt, did not try to resolve it, and told me to leave. The executive director/BCBA declined to give my clients appropriate transition time, and declined to give me time to explain to my clients why I would no longer be working with them. The executive director/BCBA and my supervising BCBA gave me ten minutes to pack up my things and I was walked out. This was not in the best interests of my clients. I had several witnesses to this incident who would be willing to provide a written, notarized, statement of this.

4. My supervising BCBA took me out of my room while I was with clients, and into her office and approached me about hearing of me being unhappy (I confided privately to a co-worker, and I was unaware that someone had been outside of the door listening). During this time, I expressed to her my concerns of the supervision she was giving not being effective and was not preparing me to become a BCBA. Specifically, I asked her if she could teach and give us work aligning with the task list, and individualize supervision for all supervisees needs instead of grouping all supervisees together. I had mentioned I had completed supervision for six months before coming to this company, and I was ready to challenge myself and gain more skill sets to become a BCBA with her support. She replied, "That is not what we do here." I know supervision is to teach, guide, and prepare us to become a BCBA, and that is what supervision should provide—contrary to what she told me.

It sounds as though there are some serious problems with regard to supervision here.

During this time, I mentioned unethical conduct, and my supervising BCBA said simply she and the company would try to be better. Not even a week later, I was again given a fraudulent supervising hours form to sign.

I feel defeated and I'm desperate to find a solution to this.

You seem like a nice, honest, ethical person and do not deserve to be treated this way.

The fraudulent supervision practices would include 5.0, 5.04, 5.05, and 5.06.

5.0 Behavior Analysts as Supervisors
When behavior analysts are functioning as supervisors, they must take full responsibility for all facets of this undertaking.

5.04 Designing Effective Supervision and Training
Behavior analysts ensure that supervision and trainings are behavior-analytic in content, effectively and ethically designed, and meet the requirements for licensure, certification, or other defined goals.

5.05 Communication of Supervision Conditions
Behavior analysts provide a clear written description of the purpose, requirements, evaluation criteria, conditions, and terms of supervision prior to the onset of the supervision.

5.06 Providing Feedback to Supervisees
a) *Behavior analysts design feedback and reinforcement systems in a way that improves supervisee performance.*
b) *Behavior analysts provide documented, timely feedback regarding the performance of a supervisee on an ongoing basis. (See also, 10.05 Compliance with BACB Supervision and Coursework Standards).*

You cannot report the company, only individual behavior analysts, so you would need to identify the BCBA who was your designated supervisor to file a Notice against. (This would be the person with the fraudulent forms.) The Notice form asks for documentation so you will have to gather any documentation or notes that you have plus the notarized statements from the other RBTs that you mentioned in order to make your case.

Hopefully, you are in an area where there are other agencies where you can go and be welcomed and receive the kind of supervision that will move you forward in your career.

##

One month later . . .
    I wanted to let you know I started with a new company and it is absolutely wonderful!
    I am so grateful this experience has worked out for the better. Thank you for all your help with my questions.

It is difficult to believe that an allegedly ABA company, headed by a BCBA executive director, could be in such complete disregard of section 5.0 of our Code of Ethics. This honest, ethical RBT was forced to violate the Code, did not receive *actual* supervision, was denied access to his supervision forms (which were fraudulent) and was then summarily discharged after offering a 30-day-notice. If you find yourself in a situation like this, be sure to keep all of your supervision documentation in a safe place in case you need it.

ETHICS QUESTION #52—RESPONSE FROM THE ETHICIST

If an RBT is listing herself as a "behavior analyst" on social media (e.g. Facebook and LinkedIn), it seems that this violates code 10.07.

Yes, this would be a violation of 10.07.

10.07 Discouraging Misrepresentation by Non-Certified Individuals RBT
Behavior analysts report non-certified (and, if applicable, non-registered) practitioners to the appropriate state licensing board and to the BACB if the practitioners are misrepresenting BACB certification or registration status.

I have notified this RBT (who reports that she will take the BCBA exam the next time it is scheduled) that this label should be changed on her social media and anywhere else.

Ideally, more people would be vigilant and take action like this.

This RBT was also involved in a recent situation in which I reported a BCBA who provided a falsified 40-hour RBT Course certificate and falsified the completion of an RBT Competency Assessment.
In that case, I reported the BCBA to the BACB, but didn't report the applicant.

> Hopefully, action was taken by the Board.

Why not? RBTs come under the Code of Ethics.

I instead provided education and feedback to the applicant. That applicant is now an RBT under yet another BCBA. (1) If this now registered RBT responds to me and changes her status, do I still need to report her to the BACB?

No, if she responds to you and changes her status, this means she has responded to your informal attempt to alleviate the situation and she does not need to be reported.

(2) If she does not respond to me and does not change her status, should I contact her current BCBA supervisor or file a report with the BCBA or both?

File a report. You are not required to notify her current BCBA; however, you can do this as a courtesy.

It is unfortunate that ethical behavior analysts must stay vigilant with regard to other individuals who would like to trade on the good name of behavior analysis and pass themselves off as registered (RBT) or certified (BCBA, BCBA-D). In order to protect our very valuable *brand*, we need to remain alert at all times for posers and pretenders who attempt to mislead the public into thinking that they are experts on behavior analysis. When people who are not qualified provide behavioral services, the result can be harm to our vulnerable clients and damage to our field's hard-earned reputation.

ETHICS QUESTION #53—RESPONSE FROM THE ETHICIST

I am a BCBA. I am also a mother to a child with an ASD diagnosis. My son is doing amazing (he had received 25–40 hours per week of ABA from the age of 2–6 and had mastered out of all areas of the VB-MAPP except social a few years ago).

Congratulations on your son's excellent progress!

Basically, his biggest impairments are his social skills, and executive functioning skills; he has some fine-motor delays, and speech/articulation issues for which he sees a speech therapist. He does not engage in challenging behaviors (aggression, SIB, etc.) and he is a very well behaved, and respectful child.

This is also very good.

Because I want to be his mom, not his BCBA, I recently sought out ABA services from XYZ Company for the purposes of working on his social/executive functioning deficits, and to provide school consultation and observations. His school will not let me observe him because I am his mother, but will allow a hired BCBA to come in to observe and offer recommendations. To clarify; he isn't having significant behavior challenges at school, but some minor noncompliance that I believe is being reinforced by the paraprofessional working with him. I hoped that if we got a BCBA, the BCBA would be able to observe and make sure the school paraprofessional is fading prompts, and challenging him enough.

My ethics concern is regarding the BCBA from XYZ Company that was assigned to us. I will try to explain as well as I can below:

1. First, the BCBA that was assigned to us is new and just passed her exam a few months ago. This BCBA came to my home for the intake interview and she had her supervisor on her iPad (on FaceTime or Skype) because she is not yet credentialed with insurance. The BCBA that was on Skype did not say a word the entire time, and it appeared as if he wasn't even paying attention to our conversation and was only there for the purpose of billing. This felt wrong to me, but I am not sure if it violates any ethical guidelines.

   This is a violation of 1.04 (c).

2. Second, the BCBA that came to my home did not spend any time with my son (except for a few minutes when she arrived and said hello to him). She relied solely on the parent questionnaire on the XYZ Company Portal, and questions during the intake interview to develop his treatment plan. She did not do any direct assessment, data collection, or observation of him.

   This is a clear violation of 3.0 and 3.01.

   During this intake, I did inform her that I am also a BCBA. We discussed XYZ's new arrival in my town as a satellite office that does only in-home services (with an actual clinic in the nearby city). The BCBA informed me that they are planning to open a clinic as soon as they have enough clients. She stated that my son was one of the last ones she needed in order to have enough to open their clinic.

   MO just revealed.

   About two weeks later, this BCBA informed me that she had gotten an authorization from my insurance company and returned to my home to review his treatment plan (this was three days ago).

3. The BCBA informed me that she had requested, and been approved for 25 hours/week in his authorization from my insurance company. I was very surprised by this, and had asked her why she had asked for 25 hours per week.

   This is a clear violation of 2.09 (b) "appropriate amount and level of service . . . " as well as 4.02.

   4.02 Involving Clients in Planning and Consent
   Behavior analysts involve the client in the planning of and consent for behavior-change programs.

She stated that she based this on when we were available, and how many hours my child could get in during that time. The schedule she planned for my son was that since he would be at school from 8:50am–3:30pm M–F (we get home at 3:45), that she would like to have a therapist come to our home M–F from 4 or 4:30 until 8pm, and on Saturdays to have two sessions back to back with two different therapists. This was highly concerning to me, and throughout the conversation, she was entirely focused on him getting the full 25 hours a week. She again mentioned that they now have enough clients to open a clinic, and that she believes it will be done by December. (I feel that it is important here to contrast that my professional opinion, as a BCBA, would be to provide my son with a Focused ABA program, and that two to three afternoon sessions per week would be an appropriate amount of services for his level of need and deficits.)

There are sufficient violations here to warrant pushback on your part.

It appears you are correct.

4. My feeling here is that the BCBA is simply trying to meet her quota. Once she has so many hours/clients, they can then open the clinic. I felt that this was more of her agenda than providing appropriate ABA to my son.
5. I informed the BCBA that I felt that the number of hours that she has recommended was too many, I did not feel that would be appropriate for him, and that I feel it is much too high for a highly functioning kid with his skillset.

Is this in writing?

She gave me a guilt trip and informed me that research shows that less than 25 hours a week is not as effective, and she continued to try and convince me to schedule him for 25 hours.

This is a rookie mistake. The BCBA seems to not have enough experience to know the context for this recommendation; clearly it is not appropriate for your child's needs.

I informed her that I did not feel it is appropriate for my child to not have any free-time during his weekdays, and that it seems inappropriate to schedule any kid for every free moment that they have during the week. I clarified with her that what she was recommending, which was to barely have any down-time, and then be in therapy from 4–8pm, then go to bed at 8:30. I explained that this doesn't allow for family time, or play time with his siblings, etc. I was significantly concerned over her recommendation and the pressure she was placing on me as a parent (and fellow BCBA). I mainly am concerned for parents that do not know better and are pressured to accept this highly inappropriate schedule because of her misquoted data regarding ABA not being effective if it is under 25 hours per week.

This is an additional reason for pushing back on this. From what you have described already, you have completed the requisite "informal resolution" section 7.02 (c) of the Code. You can proceed to 7.02 (d) and file a "Notice" with the Board.

7.02 Ethical Violations by Others and Risk of Harm [RBT]
7.02 (d) If the matter meets the reporting requirements of the BACB, behavior analysts submit a formal complaint to the BACB.

6. I also responded to her pressure by saying that I can understand her recommending 25 hours/week if he needed a comprehensive ABA program, if he had significant behavior challenges, high levels of skill deficits, or if he hadn't had years of ABA already, and I re-informed her that he has already done that with his 40 hours a week of Comprehensive ABA between the ages of 2–6, and I was seeking a Focused ABA program for his social skills and executive functioning skills only. She looked confused and changed the topic, leaving me to believe that she does not know the difference between Focused ABA and Comprehensive ABA. This also was highly concerning to me that she is not familiar with the Practice Guidelines the BACB established.

Do you have this in writing? If not, you need to carefully document this before you forget exactly what you said.

7. In addition, the treatment plan goals that she had selected for my son were not appropriate. She selected skills that he had mastered four years ago, and when I informed her that he already does that, she would say something along the lines of "well, we will just start with these skills and then master them out, and move on from there." Instead of assessing him properly, or collecting baseline data on her target skills (for acquisition), it feels like she was just guessing and there was no data behind the targets that were selected. She even had chosen noncompliance as a target, even though I had informed her that he is very compliant and that we do not have behavior challenges at home.

All of Section 3.0 "Assessment" is relevant here.

8. The BCBA also told me that she would need to do two to three hours of parent training with me each month. I asked her if this is an insurance requirement, or if it is from XYZ Company. She told me it is from XYZ Company. I said I understand the importance of parent training, but I am a BCBA, and feel that it is not necessary to train me on ABA techniques to use with my son; yet she insisted that it was required. I do not feel that this is right for her to have three more billable hours per month to train me on things I already know how to do. It just seems wrong to me.

Yes, this is a violation of 4.01–4.04 of the Code.

9. Lastly, I had asked her if they use the AFLS, and named some other protocols, and she said, no, that they use their own (that XYZ Company had developed), and this also felt wrong to me. I feel that whatever protocols are most applicable to a client should be used, and not just the one that the company developed. For example, I use the ABLLS-R on certain clients, and the VB-MAPP on others depending on which is more appropriate for that particular client.

This is correct; this is a violation of 3.03 (b).

I apologize for the length of this email. What I really am trying to find out is what do I do from here? I know that as a BCBA, I am supposed to go directly to the individual (BCBA), bring it to her attention and try to resolve the matter prior to reporting to the BACB.

Yes, going to the BCBA first is the general procedure and you have done that.

I feel comfortable doing this, but I don't know if I am supposed to act as a BCBA, or as a concerned parent . . .

In this case, you are operating as a very well-educated parent.

that feels like a BCBA is trying to take advantage of getting the most billable hours possible to meet her quota.

This is unethical in so many ways and it borders on fraud. The insurance company could also be informed about this.

In addition, I want to express that I feel that there is a huge problem that I have observed over the years where BCBAs become certified, and do not really know what they are doing. My experience this week was truly similar to those I have read about on some parent support groups (and I had thought were exaggerated, or made up) where parents express their dissatisfaction with ABA/BCBA's. This BCBA really was just like a robot in an ABA factory trying to meet quotas on billable hours . . . and not really considering the actual needs of the client, or using data to make decisions as to what would be best for this client as an individual, and as a human being, and not just as a tool for billing 25 hours per week.

This is an image that is hard to get out of one's head.

Jon S. Bailey: "I have been talking about the clash of values between capitalism and ABA for a number of years. Working to meet a quota, payroll or a profit margin can warp a person's values so that all they can see is dollar signs and lose track of their primary purpose which is to help our clients meet their goals while keeping within the lines established by our Code of Ethics."

Can you give me some direction from here? How should I address this?

You have met the requirement for an informal solution but if you do not agree, then you could re-formulate what you have here and put it in writing to the XYZ Company and request a meeting to resolve the issues.

##

Five months later . . .

I thought you would like to know that I did decide to file a Notice of Alleged Violation against this BCBA. I am not permitted to give you the details but I can say that they ruled in my favor and that the BCBA will have to undergo some additional training.

This well-educated parent, a BCBA herself, understood the Code of Ethics and best practices in ABA and realized that the recommendations that were being made for her child were inappropriate, and that there were specific elements of the Code that were being violated as well. She was able to cite those items and essentially just needed backup from an ethicist to validate her position. It is important to note that she attempted to work this out with the BCBA therapist who came to her home to no avail. In the end, she decided that filing a Notice was the best course of action in line with 7.02 (d).

ETHICS QUESTION #54—RESPONSE FROM THE ETHICIST

I am writing about an ethical issue that has come to my attention since relocating and joining a new company. I appreciate any guidance you may be able to provide.

As I have started taking over cases at my new company I have come across an issue that pertains to use and dissemination of Intellectual Property.

The prior BCBA (whose cases I am taking over) has completed a variety of assessments including the ABLLS-R, VB-MAPP, and Essentials for Living with clients. During the transition, she provided electronic copies of the scoring grids but not the protocol books for the clients. I emailed a request to the BCBA requesting the protocol books, but she did not respond.

Is your owner a BCBA?

I reached out to the company owner (my supervisor) as I have a client who is in need of an assessment. Her initial response via email was, "I have blank protocols. You can make copies and use what you need."

As this is inappropriate . . . (in my understanding of Intellectual Property and copyright laws), I responded with, "It is my understanding that since these are copyrighted materials they are not licensed for duplication. Is that correct? If you have a different understanding or agreement with the developer(s), I would be very interested in learning more. Otherwise, if we don't want to deal with those complications, can we brainstorm other solutions to accessing the needed assessments?"

It is actually illegal.

My goal essentially was to bring to her attention the issues of copying copyrighted material and to identify solutions—either purchase the protocols appropriately or to identify/develop assessment strategies that do not involve copyrighted material. She responded by saying we would talk about it in person when we met. During that meeting, she shared the VB-MAPP Guidebook, but said she would have to get the protocol from home. I said this would be fine because we had a staff meeting coming up and I could get it then.

After this meeting, I reached out to the publisher of the VB-MAPP . . .

In addition to the publisher contact you spoke to, you should contact Dr. Mark Sundberg, the author/researcher of all of this material.

regarding appropriate usage as I wanted to make sure I was correct in my understanding prior to making any statements/additional requests for individual protocols. He was very helpful in clarifying my presented questions. From those email conversations, he confirmed my statement that making copies of protocol books was inappropriate . . .

It is actually illegal, a violation of Intellectual Property, and a violation of the BACB Ethical Code 8.02 (a).

8.02 Intellectual Property[RBT]
(a) *Behavior analysts obtain permission to use trademarked or copyrighted materials as required by law. This includes providing citations, including trademark or copyright symbols on materials, that recognize the intellectual property of others.*

and he addressed some other usage concerns including the Excel grid and a violation of the BACB Ethics Code if the person involved is a behavior analyst.

My company met this morning in a staff meeting. Three BCBAs—including myself—were present along with four RBTs. At the end of the meeting, my supervisor presented me with a protocol book for my client. She stated that if I "needed" each client to have their own protocol she would likely purchase the application rather than books. I said I appreciated that and would be happy to work with either the book or application, whichever the company felt was most appropriate. She then went on to say that the company did not typically purchase a protocol for each student. I stated that I would be more comfortable since the cases would be under my certification if each child had his or her own protocol as it was an issue of Intellectual Property and making copies is not permitted. Her response was "yes, technically it is, but" and turned to a newly hired RBT in the meeting and asked if they (her former company) provided a protocol book for each child to which the RBT responded "no." I also mentioned that should an issue arise from a family against the company, that a copied assessment would not be considered an appropriate diagnostic tool for services in court (based on my conversations with the publisher). She agreed but said it would be unlikely to happen. I agreed that while unlikely, it would still be in the company's best interest to have individualized protocols for each client. I followed up with it also being a part of our Ethical Code. Again, she responded "yes, technically but" and followed with a rough timeframe of it being 20 years that she has been working in this manner with no negative consequences. The RBT that she had turned to previously then also stated, "yeah, but the code changes all the time." I was a bit in shock by the blatant disregard for the code and the conversation ended with that. I thanked her for the protocol book and wished everyone a good day since the meeting was over.

They do not seem to have been trained on the Ethical Code, or they don't care about it.

My questions/comments are as follows:

1. Based on the information collected from the publisher contact and in review of the BACB Professional and Ethical Compliance Code, it appears as if there is a violation.
   a. Specifically, it appears that the owner is practicing unethically by photocopying copyright protocols and encouraging staff to (8.02a).

   Yes. The publisher should have their attorney send a Cease and Desist letter immediately to the owner/supervisor.

   This is correct.

   b. Additionally, there may be grounds for 2.10—Documenting Professional Work and Research, as a new BCBA to the case is unable to transition services smoothly due to the lack of documentation of the assessment; and 2.11—Records and Data as the prior assessments were not "maintained, and stored" appropriately.

   Both have violated the Code.

   Would this be more of an issue with the BCBA who transitioned off the cases, the owner, or both?

2. Regarding the steps to addressing an alleged violation, it is my understanding that the first step is to discuss the concern with the person committing the violation and try to correct for it. I feel I have done this with the owner of the company through the email conversations as well as the discussion in the meeting.

   Yes, you have met this requirement.

   These did not result in what I would consider "resolved" outcomes. While she is willing to purchase protocol books for me, the owner's overall approach still seems to be making copies and supporting that decision in front of her staff.

   If you are going to report the owner (or anyone) to the Board, you will need evidence of each violation.

3. Additionally, I am disappointed that despite knowing that it is inappropriate to copy these materials, the owner is advocating that we do so in front of the staff. It is also unfortunate that this is the model being set forth for those she is supervising RBT's and those seeking certification as a BCBA. This is possibly a violation of 6.0—Responsibility to the Profession of Behavior Analysis, and possibly 5.0—Supervision or 10.05—Compliance with Supervision.

   See 7.01 in the Code. The owner is not promoting an ethical culture at this company.

   Yes, certainly.

4. Based on the information provided, do you think this would warrant a filing of a complaint with the BACB?

At this point, and based on the owner's comments during this morning's meeting, I am planning on doing so for the owner.

I would appreciate more clarification on the role of the BCBA who transferred her cases to me—perhaps she asked and the owner told her to copy protocols so she was following company directives?

Assuming she's a BCBA?

If you are a BCBA and told to do something that violates the Code of Ethics the answer is, "No, I won't do that . . ."

a. If there are any other remedial steps between those that I have taken (discussing it directly with the owner, bringing the code to her attention) prior to filing a complaint, I would like to take that first.

Not necessary, this is blatant and long standing.

b. If there are any steps I should take with the BCBA who transitioned off the cases, I would appreciate guidance to that as well.

Yes, file a Notice.

5. Following the staff meeting this morning, I am left with the feeling that the culture set forth by this business is one that is not as committed to upholding the ethical practices our field strives for and despite the attempted resolution, is unlikely to make a significant change in practices.

This is a very unethical environment.

Good decision.

As such, I feel I must separate myself from this business and resign.

This is very unfortunate since I recently relocated about 900 miles to take this position.

Would it be appropriate to professionally address my reason for leaving being the ethical concerns I have?

Yes, certainly.

Also, if I file a complaint, should I notify the owner?

No, she will just brush it off as an idle threat. She will receive a copy of your Notice from the Board and have a chance to respond.

6. I only started a few months ago so it will be a quick departure, but I think it would be in my and the client's best interest for me to resign now, rather than wait months to avoid interrupting or discontinuing services. I plan to offer four weeks to support a transition plan.

I only work part-time for the company, so I feel that this is an appropriate length of time.

This is the standard period, 30-days.

One day later . . .

The blasé approach the owner had to commenting that it was part of the Code was very disheartening.

I do have a follow-up question with respect to the data to support the report violation. The website mentions affidavits. Since other staff were present at the staff meeting this morning, I would like to reach out to them. Having never done this I am unsure how to approach the request. Do you have any guidance in that?

You will need to choose carefully who to approach since if the owner hears about this it could be bad for anyone who cooperates with you. So, find a like-minded person and meet with them away from the agency property, remind them of the meeting and gauge their reaction. If you get any hint that they did not have the same reaction as you, drop

the inquiry, go into your social skills mode, and then wrap it up. If you do get a positive reaction, tell the person of your deep concern and ask if they would support you in filing a Notice with the Board. If yes, ask if they would write a short statement for you verifying what you heard. Ideally, the statement from your witness should be notarized (again off property).

If there is any chance you received formal notice that you were not to contact any staff of the facility, proceed on your own with filing with the Board without contacting staff.

##

One day later . . .

Thank you for the additional info. I agree that other staff will likely be hesitant to participate as they are financially dependent on their position with the company. It took longer than expected, but I did receive a response regarding my resignation. The owner still denies inappropriate behavior and claims the electronic grid is common practice. Although I offered four weeks to transition, she accepted my resignation as immediate, which frankly, as long as she has the clients covered, works for me. I still plan to submit a Notice of Alleged Violation as well as continue to reach out to program authors for clarification regarding use of materials. Perhaps the authors and/or the BACB can help clarify should I have anything unclear in this matter.

As we have terminated our professional relationship, I have client materials that need to be returned to the company. I am not comfortable returning them to the office in person, but I'm not sure that mailing them would be appropriate either as they contain client info. Is there a priority mail or anything of that nature that would be appropriate to get these materials back without having to physically deliver them?

While having to resign was no doubt traumatic, you must feel a relief to be away from this situation. As to sending the materials back, I would send via a carrier where someone has to sign that the client files have been received. The U.S. Post Office version of this is Certified Mail-Return Receipt Requested.

As this writer has expressed, violating copyright law has become quite common in our field, but it certainly does not make it right or ethical under 8.02 (a) of our Code of Ethics. Companies should obey the U.S. Copyright Act of 1976 and purchase commercial materials they need for assessments, intakes, data collection, etc. Using a copy machine to print copyrighted materials denies the author(s) of their due profits from *their* Intellectual Property—basically, this is theft.

ETHICS QUESTION #55—RESPONSE FROM THE ETHICIST

I have a few questions.

1. I got assigned a new BCBA supervisor about three months ago. We met the week she started and went over the supervision contract that my old BCBA and I drew up. The new supervisor also had the sample contract that the board provides. She said she would make some changes and adjust it to fit our needs and get it back to me to sign. I just realized when organizing my supervision pages that she never did get a contract back to me to sign. This means we have no supervision contract and haven't had one for the last three months.

> This could cause trouble later.

I am an RBT but currently in my third class for my BCaBA so I am following those experience standards. Do my hours from the last three months not count? Is she at fault for this? I think she is at fault for sure. According to the BACB Experience Standards:

"DOCUMENTATION OF ONGOING SUPERVISION: The supervisee and supervisor are responsible for collecting documentation on the Experience Supervision Form during each supervisory period. One form should be completed within each supervisory period, ideally at each meeting. Backdated forms will not be accepted. The BACB reserves the right to request this documentation at any time following an individual's application to take the certification exam. This documentation should NOT be submitted with an exam application unless specifically requested by the BACB."

2. There is a BCBA who no longer works at our company. A new BCBA took over her caseload. I have been expected to work with clients that still have old behavior reduction plans. The oldest plan goes back nine months.

   When the new BCBA took over the caseload she should have reviewed all the programs and updated them as necessary; see Code 4.03 which pertains to this.

   a) Can we implement plans written by a BCBA who no longer works for us? I am guessing probably not because these plans don't include the current diagnosis of ASD and are not current on behavior.

   No, this is not acceptable.

   How long does a behavior reduction plan usually last or for how long is it valid?

   The short answer is, "It depends," but in general, a reduction plan should be reviewed by a Case Management Team at least once per month to determine if it is having the desired effect. If it is not, according to the data, it is revised and the revised program is evaluated at the end of the next month.

   b) For some of the clients I have been providing services for, the BCBA just met the parents since getting switched to these clients almost two months ago. Is this unethical?

   4.02 implies that this is done in a timely fashion but the details are not included in the Code. Decisions like this are usually left to the professional to decide. Two months is far too long; two weeks would be considered a long time. It sounds like the BCBA has too many cases and cannot keep track of them all. See Code 5.0 on Caseload size and effectiveness.

   c) I have also been told to use interventions without signed consent of new goals that are not even listed in the original plans from the previous BCBA.

   > This is not good.

   This is definitely unethical; see Code 4.04 that covers this violation.

Is this a fault of my own or the new BCBA?

> **This is the fault of the BCBA, but as an RBT you must take responsibility for the quality of the treatment. You have an obligation to operate quickly when high-quality treatment is not provided.**

Is a transition period acceptable? If yes, about how long?

> **This generally refers to the period where a client is transitioned from one BCBA to another or even outsourced to another agency. Thirty days is the standard, acceptable period for transition in our field.**

My goal here is not to get anyone in trouble. I just want to learn what is ethical and unethical before I approach my superiors about the issues I am experiencing.

> **It sounds as though you have an eye for detail and that you care about the clients and doing the right thing. You should review the BACB Code of Ethics and be prepared to talk with your BCBA (as per 7.02 of the Code) about all of this.**

##

Two weeks later . . .

So, the BCBA who I was discussing just resigned with only one day's notice from the company. She sent me an email saying she is no longer my supervising BCBA and that was it.

I'm confused as to what to do next. I filed a Notice of Alleged Violation because I do truly believe she was being unethical. I think it's unfair how my being able to practice and the clients I see are on the line due to her choices.

> **This is good that you filed the Notice.**

Since she is gone effective tomorrow, I now have other questions of an ethical nature.

1. Do I have to notify my clients' parents that I am not longer a practicing RBT since I do not have a BCBA supervisor?

   > **First, you need to inform the Board that you no longer have a Responsible Certificant to supervise you as per Code 10.05.**
   >
   > ***10.05 Compliance With BACB Supervision and Coursework Standards* RBT**
   > *Behavior analysts ensure that coursework (including continuing education events), supervised experience, RBT training and assessment, and BCaBA supervision are conducted in accordance with the BACB's standards if these activities are intended to comply with BACB standards.*
   >
   > **You can inform the parents of your situation, but be careful what you say since they may repeat it. You do not want to be accused of slander.**

2. My company is convinced that if they use the job title "behavior support specialist" for me I can carry out the plans previous BCBAs have written even though they are no longer here to monitor/update.

   > **This is not correct. You are a registered behavior technician and are required by the Board to be supervised; the job title does not matter nor does it matter that a BCBA wrote the plans. The key issue is that RBTs must, under all circumstances, be supervised.**

Supervision Requirements

"The RBT will have at least one Responsible Certificant who is publicly listed in the *RBT Registry*. This certificant is responsible for ensuring the RBT is working under the supervision of a BACB certificant." From the BACB.com site.

Am I wrong in saying that just anyone can't carry out interventions put in place by a BCBA with whom they no longer have contact?

Correct, see above.

##

My boss (not a behavior anything, an LCSW actually) states that since my job title at my company is a "behavior support specialist," I am required to see clients and continue with my sessions as normal.

This is not true. You are an RBT and come under the rules of the BCBA.

I was practicing and signing all documentation as a Registered Behavior Technician prior to this fiasco. 〈 *This is correct.*

Our program is divided into two parts. One part of the program deals with individuals with challenging behaviors. For the second part of the program, the client has to have an autism diagnosis. In both programs, it is required that they get a behavior support plan which includes behavior reduction goals and interventions as well as replacement and functional skills if BCBA sees fit. All plans are written by a 〈 *So far, this sounds alright.*
BCBA. The RBTs then carry out the plans with the clients.

My boss (LCSW) stated that even though I'm not practicing as an RBT (due to me not having a responsible certificate/supervisor) that I can continue as normal under the title of a "behavior support specialist."

They can change your title all they want; you are an RBT and come under the BACB Code of Ethics.

Am I allowed to be providing ABA services to these clients without supervision of a BCBA? 〈 *No.*
Is there any rule that states only RBTs can provide this type of service?

Yes, there is a rule, go to this link and read the page: www.bacb.com/rbt/

The Registered Behavior Technician^TM (RBT®) *is a paraprofessional who practices under the close, ongoing supervision of a BCBA, BCaBA, or FL-CBA. The RBT is primarily responsible for the direct implementation of behavior-analytic services. The RBT does not design intervention or assessment plans. It is the responsibility of the RBT supervisor to determine which tasks an RBT may perform as a function of his or her training, experience, and competence. The BACB certificant supervising the RBT is responsible for the work performed by the RBT on the cases they are overseeing.*

If your BCBA leaves the company and there is not another one to supervise, basically you are out of business until another one comes along.

The assumption of the BACB is that RBTs work in agencies where there are multiple BCBAs to provide supervision so that if one quits another will take over supervision seamlessly.

##

So, my boss has read the sections of the Code above and says that it only says "RBTs" and nothing states that I have to have a credential to provide ABA services to clients because the company as a whole doesn't have to abide by BACB standards. She said when I have an active supervisor, then I need to abide by the standards.

##

As if I needed more wood for this fire . . .

My supervisor said to our HR director that if I wanted her to sign off on my hours she needed a copy of all my supervision sheets (which I already gave her after each meeting) as well as my spreadsheet for her "verification purposes." Thankfully, I decided to look through all of the documentation before sending it to her. I noticed that the pre-made Excel document I downloaded was calculating the hours incorrectly; instead of doing 60 minutes, it was doing 100.

This was a very good catch; you just saved yourself a big embarrassment.

Luckily my company has to keep track of exact minutes of all direct time with clients in our state documentation system. That being said, the supervision sheets that my boss and I have both already signed provided incorrect information. I know that the forms cannot be backdated. Does that include writing out correct ones and signing them as of today?

No, but be sure to put a note somewhere that explains why you are doing this.

I don't want to provide her any false information in case there is any retaliation, nor do I want to provide the board with any false information.

That is correct on both counts.

##

I just thought you would like to know . . . the BACB told my boss that they can change my job title. As long as I don't claim to be an RBT, I can provide behavior analytic services to my clients.

##

This is unbelievable. It seems that this opens up a huge loophole for abuse. Apart from what your boss did in changing your job title, if you "claim to be an RBT" what happens, do you get fired?

##

11:00 am

In our meeting, this morning we were told that we need to let the Board know that we are not active (i.e. Voluntary inactive). I asked if they are going to pay my two $25 fees.

##

11:06 am

Now this is a different story, it is true that if you go "inactive" that you no longer come under the Code of Ethics. It was not clear that you were considering this move. Was this

the choice of your boss or your choice? And, just to clarify, your job title changed but you'll be doing the same work as you did before?

##

12:11 pm
That is correct. I would NOT like to go inactive. That is what my boss told us to do from her conversation with the BACB. She told us this morning that she needed to do that since we don't have a BCBA supervisor along with if we wished to tell the parents that we are not practicing RBTs at this time, instead as "behavior support staff."

I will be working on goals listed in their behavior support plans which is the same service I was providing to the clients prior to losing my supervisor. These are plans that were not written by the BCBA that quit. Some are from one (or in some cases, two) BCBA(s) prior.

This is also correct.

##

12:47 pm

The first requirement for inactive status is as follows:

"1. Have you read, are you in compliance with, and do you agree to continued compliance with all Behavior Analyst Certification Board ('BACB') rules and regulations, as may be revised, including, but not limited to the RBT eligibility and supervision requirements, disciplinary (professional conduct) rules, fees and application requirements?"

This means that you must still comply with the Code of Ethics. I think your boss needs to read this carefully since it means that she is putting you directly in line with a clear violation of the Code if she is going to ask you to implement behavioral programs without supervision.

##

2:50 pm
I think she will find wiggle room as what is considered a "behavioral program" and the services I am providing.

##

Regarding finding "wiggle room," this is not a good sign as a place of employment. We (behavior analysts) see "behavioral program" in a fairly broad sense from data collection, assessment, program development, program implementation, etc. Does your boss know about the BACB Task List for RBTs? If not you should share that with her. It is quite extensive:

www.bacb.com/wp-content/uploads/2017/09/161019-RBT-task-list-english.pdf

##

3:20 pm
My boss is much more of a "show me the law where it says I can't do this," type of person. Since she has contacted the BACB and they told her it was okay, I don't think this will change. I have a feeling

her response will be something like, "Well, this is what we hired her to do so if she doesn't like it she can quit."

When people try to find loopholes, and do an end-around rather than provide adequate behavioral staff, the result is often a program with a lack of ethics.

I have been searching for other employment but being in a smaller than normal area, I don't have very many options. I am continuing to look daily in hopes something comes about.
I was contemplating the idea of reporting them to the BACB as well, as a last resort.

You can't report her since she is not a behavior analyst. You would have to report her to HER licensing board.

But after hearing the BACB say that what they are doing is okay, that plan is on a temporary hold until I can gather more information.

She may have misunderstood what she was told. She seems to have been told that you could go on inactive status, but the person forgot to tell her that you would still fall under the Code and all the BACB rules and regulations.

##

12:45pm

Regarding your question about your boss trying to get around the rule that RBTs must be supervised, I contacted the BACB and received the following correspondence:

The main issue with this inquiry and the proposed workaround is that the RBT would be performing RBT duties without supervision if they became inactive. Becoming inactive would not rectify the fact that the RBT may not perform RBT duties (enumerated in the RBT Task List) without supervision; the RBT would be in violation of Section 10.05 of the Code.

What the RBT claims BACB staff advised is partly accurate, in that there is an option for an RBT to request voluntary inactive status. However, the Inactive Status Request-RBT specifies that the RBT "shall not practice as an RBT while under voluntary inactive status." Be advised, we are working on edits to further clarify this language on the request form; specifically, "practicing as an RBT" will be replaced with "engaging in activities enumerated on the RBT Task List," or something to that effect.

Feel free to share this with your boss and let me know if you have additional questions.

Every month or so a question comes along which appears to start out as simple and straightforward but then begins to expand as more questions are raised. This RBT is going out of her way to play by the rules and follow the Code of Ethics but is thwarted at every turn by her "boss" who is not a behavior analyst, knows little about that certification and virtually nothing about the RBT title and obligations. She wants primarily to save money by not having to hire a BCBA to supervise the RBTs, end of story. And, she is looking for a "workaround" by telling this RBT that with a simple change of job title the little matter of supervision can be solved. It is heartening to know that "Inactive status" cannot be used as a loophole to avoid having RBTs avoid supervision.

NOTES

1. And, of course, *supervisees*.
2. Zones of Regulation. www.zonesofregulation.com/learn-more-about-the-zones.html
3. IRS Independent contractor defined. www.irs.gov/businesses/small-businesses-self-employed/independent-contractor-defined
4. KPCC Independent contractors vs. employees: California's Supreme Court tightens the rules. www.scpr.org/news/2018/05/01/82669/independent-workers-vs-employees-california-s-supr/
5. BACB self-reporting requirements. www.bacb.com/self-reporting-requirements/
6. Ethical Principles of Psychologists and Code of Conduct, American Psychological Association, 2017. www.apa.org/ethics/code/ethics-code-2017.pdf
7. NPR the Sexual Assault Epidemic No One Talks About. www.npr.org/2018/01/08/570224090/the-sexual-assault-epidemic-no-one-talks-about
8. Mental Health Lab, New Study Emphasizes Harm of Vaccine Refusals. https://labblog.uofmhealth.org/body-work/new-study-emphasizes-harm-of-vaccine-refusals

3

Final Words

RULES TO LIVE BY

Ethical professionals don't simply operate in a random way throughout the day. Instead, they follow a few rules that will help them avoid wrong paths, face conflicts effectively, provide a level of behavior analysis service that is second to none, and have no regrets about the steps they have taken.

> **Rule #1: Be honest** with everyone. Let your prospective employer, colleagues, and clients know that you honor the Code of Ethics.
>
> **Rule #2: Be skeptical** because you will be bombarded with "exciting new treatments" on a weekly basis from parents and colleagues in other fields. The vast majority of these so-called treatments will be fads, others will turn out to be bogus, and some will be outright frauds. They will have cutesy names, beautiful websites, and claim to have research to support them, but they won't. Your first question should always be, "Is it published in *JABA*?" If the answer is no, move on and don't argue; just use what you know about extinction.
>
> **Rule #3: Read *JABA*** regularly, this is your peer-reviewed guide to successful behavioral interventions. Don't be fooled by "studies" published elsewhere.
>
> **Rule #4: Insist on data.** Don't allow yourself to listen to hearsay or believe anecdotes. Insist that your direct reports always operate with data in hand.
>
> **Rule #5: Always ask, "Can I see that?"** when you are told something that sounds unusual, strange, or too good to be true. Insist on knowing when and where it occurs and go to see it for yourself.
>
> **Rule #6: Don't gossip.** This is a demeaning habit that sends a signal to others that you are a person of poor character who is prepared to spread rumors at the expense of others.
>
> **Rule #7: "Be the Contingency**." Be prepared to resist pressure from those who would want you to relax your ethical standards and to lavish praise on those around you who are maintaining high ethical standards.

WARNING SIGNS

Know what to look for when you are interviewing for a job. Ask tough questions about ethical conduct and how employees are trained on ethics. Do you have an ethics committee? Who is the chair of the committee? How often is ethics training conducted? What are the procedures for reporting someone in the organization for an ethics violation? What is company policy on dual relationships and conflicts of interest? What is the policy on nepotism? How is caseload determined? What is the turnover among RBTs and BCBA? Is a non-compete included in your contracts? What are your procedures for supervision? Can I observe a supervision session? The answers might present strong warning signs such as, "What's an ethics committee?" "Well, my cousin is our newest RBT and she is working out great, we have lunch every Friday . . . " "We work on billable hours here and expect everyone to produce, we have a bonus system for taking on additional clients," and, "Supervision is on the honor system." "Turnover was a problem until we instituted the non-compete."

CONCEPTS THAT COUNT

Our field has as an unwritten rule that we value transparency in all aspects of behavior analysis. Parents must give **consent** to assessment and treatment plans. There are no exceptions to this, even in school systems. It is in our Code that we value **evidence-based treatments**, but we do not always make clear that we most value the **single-case research** and methodology that goes with it. We place a high value on conceptual consistency. **Conceptual consistency** is also in the Code, but apparently glossed over by some practitioners, especially those who trained in some other field first (you know who you are). Behavior analysis is all about **operant conditioning**, not counseling, not behavior therapy, not family therapy. "Stay in your lane" is an expression that captures this wise counsel; behavior analysts do behavior analysis and nothing else under the name of behavior analysis.

CREATING AND SUSTAINING AN ETHICAL CULTURE

An ethical culture starts at the top of an organization and spills and flows down through the organization. If the owner makes it clear that the purpose of the organization is to make money and that those who support that mission will be properly rewarded, it will be difficult for BCBAs to remain ethical in their practice. Greed drives shortcuts, deception, misrepresentation, and cover-ups. It is nearly impossible to start with an ethical culture if the owner or CEO does not strongly support the BACB Code of Ethics. Further, it is clear that you cannot hold *them* to the Code if they are not behavior analysts. In an ethical culture, every policy and procedure in the employee handbook is looked at through the lens of ethics. A strong ethical organization will put client welfare first and profit second. A great ethical organization will prompt and reward ethical conduct at all levels of the company and make ethics a common item on every agenda at every meeting.

References

American Psychological Association. (2017). *Ethical principles of psychologists and code of conduct.* Washington, DC: Author. Retrieved from www.apa.org/ethics/code/ethics-code-2017.pdf

ASHA position statement rapid prompting method. Retrieved from www.asha.org/policy/ps2018-00351/

BACB ASD guidelines. (2014). BACB applied behavior analysis treatment of autism spectrum disorder: Practice guidelines for healthcare funders and managers. *Behavior Analyst Certification Board.* Retrieved from www.bacb.com/wp-content/uploads/2017/09/ABA_Guidelines_for_ASD.pdf

BACB newsletter. (November 2016, April 2017). Retrieved from www.bacb.com/wp-content/uploads/1611-newsletter.pdf, www.bacb.com/wp-content/uploads/170421-newsletter.pdf

BACB self-reporting requirements. Retrieved from www.bacb.com/self-reporting-requirements/

Bailey, J. S., & Burch, M. R. (2018). *Research methods in applied behavior analysis* (2nd ed.). New York: Routledge, Taylor & Francis Group.

Carnegie, D. (1981). *How to win friends and influence people.* New York: Simon & Schuster.

Ethical Principles of Psychologists and Code of Conduct, American Psychological Association. (2017). Retrieved from www.apa.org/ethics/code/ethics-code-2017.pdf

Foxx, R. M., & Mulick, J. A. (2016). *Controversial therapies for autism and intellectual disabilities.* New York: Routledge, Taylor & Francis Group.

Individuals with disabilities education act. Retrieved from https://sites.ed.gov/idea/about-idea/

IRS independent contractor defined. Retrieved from www.irs.gov/businesses/small-businesses-self-employed/independent-contractor-defined

KPCC independent contractors vs. employees: California's Supreme Court tightens the rules. Retrieved from www.scpr.org/news/2018/05/01/82669/independent-workers-vs-employees-california-s-supr/

Mental Health Lab, New Study Emphasizes Harm of Vaccine Refusals. Retrieved from https://labblog.uofmhealth.org/body-work/new-study-emphasizes-harm-of-vaccine-refusals

NPR. The sexual assault epidemic no one talks about. Retrieved from www.npr.org/2018/01/08/570224090/the-sexual-assault-epidemic-no-one-talks-about

Todd, J. T. (2015). Old horses in new stables: Rapid prompting, facilitated communication, science, ethics, and the history of magic. In R. M. Foxx & J. A. Mulick (Eds.), *Controversial therapies for developmental disabilities: Fad, fashion, and science in professional practice* (2nd ed.), (pp. 372–409). New York: Routledge.

Zones of regulation. Retrieved from www.zonesofregulation.com/learn-more-about-the-zones.html

Index